In the same series

AJS: The history of a great motor cycle,
   by Gregor Grant

Norton Story, *by Bob Holliday*

The Story of Honda Motor Cycles,
   by Peter Carrick

The Story of BSA Motor Cycles,
   by Bob Holliday

The Story of Kawasaki Motor Cycles,
   by Peter Carrick

The story of TRIUMPH MOTOR CYCLES

Harry Louis
& Bob Currie

 Patrick Stephens Limited

First published—1975
Second edition—1978

ISBN 0 85059 311 5

Set in 10 on 11pt Times Roman by
Blackfriars Press Limited of Leicester.
Printed in Great Britain on Buccaneer
II Matt 100 gsm paper and bound by
The Garden City Press of Letchworth
for the publishers, Patrick Stephens
Limited, Bar Hill, Cambridge CB3 8EL.

Contents

Illustrations

Diagrams in text

Triumph Story in brief

1884 Siegfried Bettmann arrives in England and is employed by Kelly & Co.

1885 Formation of S. Bettmann and Co, import-export agency; Birmingham-built bicycles exported under Bettmann label.

1886 Triumph name supplants Bettmann on export bicycles.

1887 Bettmann and Co name changed to Triumph Cycle Co; Mauritz Schulte joins firm.

1889 Triumph manufactures own bicycles; company moves from London to Much Park Street, Coventry.

1897 Schulte investigates possibility of producing Hildebrand and Wolfmuller motor cycle under licence.

1898 Bettmann negotiates to make Humber motor cycle, but agreement not reached.

1902 First Triumph motor cycle, fitted with Belgian-made Minerva engine.

1905 Triumph design and make own 3 hp engine.

1906 Horizontal-spring front fork introduced.

1907 Move to Priory Street, Coventry; 3½ hp engine supplants 3 hp model; annual production reaches 1,000 units; Bettmann elected to Coventry City Council.

1908 Jack Marshall wins single-cylinder class of Isle of Man TT race, and makes fastest lap.

1909 Production up to 3,000 machines a year.

1910 Albert Catt covers 2,000 miles in six days; magneto ignition introduced.

1913 First (experimental) vertical twin; two-stroke 225 cc Junior model introduced; Bettmann elected mayor of Coventry.

1914 Introduction of Model H 500 cc, with Sturmey-Archer gearbox and clutch, and chain-cum-belt transmission; 30,000 of these machines supplied to British and allied armies between 1914 and 1919.

1919 Schulte leaves company; Claude V. Holbrook joins as general manager.

1920 First all-chain-transmission Triumph, the Model SD; Triumph gearbox fitted.

1921 Introduction of Ricardo-developed 500 cc four-valve engine for racing and roadster models.

1923 Unit-construction 350 cc Model LS announced; cars go into production.

1924 Internal-expanding brakes fitted to chain-driven models.

1925 Mass-produced Model P, priced at £42 17s 6d, causes sensation.

1927 Two-valve ohv TT model evolved from Vic Horsman's Brooklands racer.

1928 First saddle tanks introduced on some models.

1929 Production reaches 30,000 a year; link with TWN in Germany severed.

1931 Smallest Triumph so far, the 175 cc Model X two-stroke.

1932 Val Page joins company as designer; Silent Scout models introduced; bicycle manufacture disposed of to Coventry Bicycles.

1933 Cheapest-ever Triumph, the 98 cc Gloria-Villiers at £16 16s; the 650 cc vertical twin designed by Val Page awarded the Maudes Trophy for achieving observed 500 miles in 500 minutes.

1934 New Page-designed range of single-cylinder models, together with his 650 cc vertical twin, the Model 6/1; Allan Jefferies joins competition team; name changed to Triumph Co Ltd.

1935 Model 5/10 racer added to range; new car-manufacturing plant acquired at Foleshill Road, Coventry; proposal to close Priory Street plant and stop motor-cycle production.

1936 Jack Sangster takes over Priory Street works and forms Triumph Engineering Co Ltd, with Edward Turner as general manager and chief designer; Val Page leaves to join BSA; designer Bert Hopwood joins Triumph; introduction of Tiger 70, 80 and 90 sports machines.

1937 Turner-designed 500 cc Speed Twin introduced; Brooklands test of three Tiger machines wins Maudes Trophy; registered office at Dale Street Coventry.

1938 Much Park Street, original Triumph works in Coventry, closed.

1939 Tiger 100 twin marketed. Maudes Trophy won for third time.

1940 Unit-construction 350 cc twin, the 3TW, accepted for military purposes; Priory Street works destroyed in Coventry blitz.

1941 Temporary premises acquired at Cape of Good Hope, Warwick; work on new factory at Meriden starts; Edward Turner moves to BSA.

1942 Meriden factory opened; single-cylinder 350 cc 3HW model in production for military use.

1944 Edward Turner returns to Triumph, as managing director.

1945 Post-war civilian range announced — 3H, 3T, Speed Twin and Tiger 100.

1946 Ernie Lyons wins the Senior Manx Grand Prix on prototype of GP model.

1947 Bert Hopwood leaves to join Norton.

1948 TR5 Trophy model announced.

1949 First 650 cc vertical twin, the 6T Thunderbird, announced.

1951 Triumph Corporation in America starts operations; Triumph sold to BSA group for about £2½ million.

1953 Terrier 150 cc model introduced.

1956 Jack Sangster becomes chairman of BSA group; American Johnny Allen covers flying mile at 214.4 mph.

1957 Unit-construction 350 cc 3TA Twenty-One introduced.

1959 First Bonneville 650 cc T120 announced.

1960 BSA group makes record profit of nearly £3.5 million in centenary year; chairman Jack Sangster hands over to Eric Turner.

1961 Bert Hopwood rejoins Triumph.

1962 Bill Johnson, with a streamlined Bonneville, sets an FIM-recognised world record of 224.57 mph; Doug Hele joins Triumph from Norton.

1964 Edward Turner, managing director of the motorcycle division of BSA group, retires, but continues as BSA director.

1966 Bob Leppan, using two 650 cc engines in a streamliner, raises the American record to 245.6 mph.

1967 Edward Turner retires from BSA board of directors; Gary Nixon, on a 500 cc Triumph, wins Daytona 200-mile race.

1968 Trident 750 cc three-cylinder model introduced.

1970 Malcolm Uphill, riding a Trident, wins 750 cc class of the Production Machine TT.

1971 BSA group discloses loss of over £8 million; Lord Shawcross becomes chairman; Trident, ridden by Ray Pickrell, wins 750 cc Production Machine TT at over 100 mph, and Tony Jefferies, also on a Trident, wins first Formula 750 TT at 102.85 mph.

1972 BSA group loses £3.3 million; Pickrell, on Tridents, wins both Production (101.61 mph) and Formula 750 (105.68 mph) TTs.

1973 BSA group virtually bankrupt and taken over by Norton Villiers Triumph with an investment of nearly £4.9 million from government funds and Dennis Poore as chairman (July); closure of Triumph Meriden plant announced (September) and start of work-in; Tony Jefferies, on Trident, wins Production TT.

1974 Start of Trident production at the Small Heath factory (March); Slippery Sam, the Trident used by Pickrell and Jefferies to win their Production TTs, first for the fourth time, with Mick Grant riding; Bert Hopwood retires.

1975 Meriden workers' co-operative formed with government loan of £4.2 million (March); Trident NT160 model with electric starter introduced; Dave Croxford and Alex George win ten-lap Production TT at 99.6 mph to register Slippery Sam's fifth win in the class, with record lap at 102.82 mph.

1976 Closure of the Small Heath factory ends Trident production (January). To NVT order, production of single-carburettor Tiger TR7RV is resumed at Meriden. Cash flow problems lead Meriden Co-operative to take on assembly of 125 cc Moto-Guzzi two-strokes, and Puch exercising machines.

1977 Government rescue plan for Meriden includes £½ million loan, to purchase Triumph name and sales rights from NVT. Working capital is provided by GEC, which buys 2,000 machines in stock, for £1 million; GEC also offers management and technical expertise, and Lord Stokes, former British Leyland chairman, assists in overseas sales organisation. Independence from NVT finally arranged in May. First new model from Meriden Motor Cycles Ltd is limited-edition, Silver Jubilee Bonneville.

Introduction by Dennis Poore

Chairman, Norton Villiers Triumph Ltd

EVER SINCE the first model was assembled by the loving hands of its enthusiastic makers in 1902, Triumph machines have occupied a particular niche in the forefront of British motor cycling. Nurtured by the skills and energies of many, though most prominently by the genius of Edward Turner, the firm went from strength to strength when others were falling by the wayside in ever-increasing numbers. Its zenith came, perhaps, in the mid-1960s, when Triumph fame had spread throughout the United States, particularly on the dirt race-tracks where its name rang from coast to coast.

On Edward Turner's retirement, the management became the responsibility of others within the BSA organisation, many of whom were distracted by non-motor cycle interests in the group, and the sad decline began. By 1972 BSA bankruptcy loomed close and I was honoured to be invited by the British Government to mount a rescue operation to avoid the indignity of the last rites.

Drastic surgery was essential to preserve the soul. Unfortunately, the plan became a *cause célèbre* in the history of British industrial relations, and politics took the place of the spirit of motor cycling. Triumph success was originally built on the hard, proven merit of engineering designs which had already lasted without major change for over 25 years. To avert the decline, a rejuvenation of the engineering base was required, not obstructive

political warfare. In the words of Kipling:

England is a garden and such gardens are not made
By singing, 'Oh, how beautiful,' and sitting in the shade.

Harry Louis and Bob Currie are to be congratulated on setting out the tale of Triumph and of Disaster alike. Posterity will be grateful for the dedication they have brought to the task.

Acknowledgements

BOB CURRIE AND I have each spent most of our years in motor cycling and have always followed the fortunes of Triumph very closely. Yet we could not have completed this book without the help of innumerable good friends who willingly pointed the way on research or in establishing facts.

Among them were Ivor Davies, Doug Hele, Victor Horsman, Allan Jefferies, John Joiner, Hugh Palin, Harry Perrey, Tyrell Smith, Jack Wickes and Leslie Williams. In particular, for the preparation of Chapter 11 we were fortunate enough to enjoy the co-operation of Denis McCormack, of Maryland, who built up the highly successful Triumph Corporation in America. No one else could have provided so much inside information. We are grateful to them all.

A remarkable contribution came from Jack Sangster, that far-seeing, astute businessman who, when the original Triumph company decided to concentrate solely on car production in 1936, bought the ailing motor-cycle side and transformed it into the flourishing enterprise we were to know for the next 30 years. He studiously vetted the chapters on company history, adding a wealth of facts and figures hitherto unpublished. No thanks can do justice to his kindly guidance.

The illustrations are a unique collection. The pictures came from a variety of sources but by far the majority from the archives of *Motor Cycle*, the London-based journal which has served motor cycling so well for over 70 years. We are indebted to *Motor Cycle* for permission to reproduce those pictures and all the line drawings.

Finally, our thanks to Dennis Poore, chairman of Norton Villiers Triumph Ltd, for suggesting that the book should be published and for encouragement while it was being prepared. The writing was done during the dramatic period, related in Chapter 5, when the future of Triumph at the Meriden plant was being decided by political expediency rather than his commercial acumen.

In spite of the almost unbelievable frustrations and workload forced on him, Dennis Poore managed to find time to interest himself in the way the book was shaping.

London, 1977   Harry Louis

Authors' notes

ALTHOUGH in the appropriate place the text makes the point clear, it is perhaps as well to emphasise that, from 1936, the manufacturers of Triumph motor cycles were in no way connected with the manufacturers of Triumph motor cars.

It is not possible to record the history of Triumph motor cycles from 1951, when the company became part of the BSA group, without trespassing to some extent on the BSA story, since the merger made it inevitable that the fortunes of the two companies were interwoven. Similarly, from 1973 onward, minor references to Norton are necessary.

Certain repetitions have been permitted to make easier reading for those who pick up this book from time to time and may have forgotten what has gone before, and for those who may prefer to peruse sections or chapters at random rather than in sequence.

Chapter 1

The man from Nuremberg

OUT IN THE GREY November world of 1884, beyond the window of the London lodging house, iron-shod wheels echoed sharply in the cobbled street. Edging aside the heavy curtain, the young German followed the progress of the home-going coster's cart through the pool of yellow light from the gas street lamp. Then, turning, he once more scanned the *Daily Telegraph*.

For a fortnight and more, ever since his arrival in England, by way of Paris, 21-year-old Siegfried Bettmann had chased up every advertised job that seemed even remotely suitable though, so far, without success. This time, he told himself, it would be different. The job seemed to be tailor-made for him.

'Youth wanted for publishing house. Knowledge of German essential. Salary 25s weekly. Apply to Kelly and Co, Strand, London.'

Bettmann was no penniless immigrant. Back home in Nuremberg his father, Mayer Bettmann, was estate manager to an important Bavarian landowner, and he had been able to provide Siegfried with an above-average standard of education. He spoke English and French as well as his native German. He had been allowed his fling in Paris; now it was time he got on with the serious job of earning a living.

The job at Kelly was not particularly exciting, but at least it brought in a steady wage while he considered which field best suited his talents. Then, as now, Kelly were publishers of a wide range of trade and street directories. Young Bettmann was given the task of extracting, from foreign journals, lists of manufacturers in various fields for inclusion in the Kelly publications.

To obtain details of their products he had to write to the firms concerned and, in that way, got to know something of the White Sewing Machine Co of Cleveland, Ohio. (Later, White took on the manufacture of steam cars and commercial vehicles, and were responsible during the Second World War for the well-known White half-track carrier.)

The White company had a European office in Queen Victoria Street, London, and, after a spell of the Kelly drudgery, Bettmann wangled a better-paid post with the American firm. At first he dealt with inquiries from the Continent by correspond-

ence, but soon he was appointed commercial traveller with, as his territory, much of Europe and a large slice of North Africa.

'I acquired a lot of new customers for the company,' he recalled many years later in an unpublished autobiography, 'and many of them became life-long friends who supported me in my subsequent undertakings.'

The first of those undertakings was now not so far away, for a quarrel with White's London manager, George Sawyer, left Bettmann out of a job again. It was a turning point in his career because he resolved that, henceforth, he would be his own boss. So, late in 1885, the import-export agency of S. Bettmann and Co was established at Holborn Viaduct, London. However the 'company' bit was as yet imaginary; it was just a piece of window dressing to impress clients.

Bettmann got in touch with various overseas manufacturers offering to represent them in Britain but, with the exception of that for Biesolt and Locke, a firm of sewing-machine makers in Meissen, Germany, the agencies failed to prosper. On the export side, though, he fared better.

By 1885 the bicycle boom was well under way and British-built machines were in great demand abroad. Bettmann joined the bonanza by ordering from William Andrews, a Birmingham maker, a batch of 'own-transfer' machines. These sold reasonably well on the Continent, but it was soon clear that a Bettmann label had its limitations. He decided that he needed a catchier name – one that would be recognisable in most European languages. How about Triumph? The same word, he reasoned, was understood in English, French and German.

The Triumph bicycles remained export-only at first, but as business expanded the sewing-machine side was pushed into the background. Very soon Triumph bicycles were appearing on the home market and, to present an image more in keeping with the product, S. Bettmann and Co became the Triumph Cycle Co.

But there were even more momentous happenings ahead when, in 1887, Bettmann took on as junior partner another young German, Mauritz Johann Schulte. If Bettmann was the business brain, Schulte was the far-sighted engineer, and the first major decision of the partners was that, if they were to get to grips with a competitive world, they would have to manufacture on their own account. Moreover, as Coventry was the place where exciting things were happening in the bicycle field, the projected Triumph works should be in that city.

On a capital of only £650 (of which £500 had been provided by Bettmann's parents and £150 by Schulte's relations) it was a tall order. Nevertheless, Schulte set out to look for suitable premises, leaving Bettmann to carry on the London end of the business.

Schulte soon found a likely site in a vacant factory at Earls Court, Coventry (a grand-sounding address which was, in truth, a narrow entry off Much Park Street, in the centre of the town). Not only would the owner lease the premises but, even better, he was prepared to invest money in the venture.

That owner was Alderman Albert Tomson, who had started in Coventry's once-thriving ribbon industry at the age of 12. An active local politician, he was to be seven times Mayor of Coventry, and a founder of the city's technical institute, before his illustrious career was over.

Though the Much Park Street works now became the Triumph headquarters, the London office was retained under the management of yet another young German, Philip Schloss. He, too, came from Nuremberg, and was a traveller for a toy firm, before he gave up that job to join Bettmann. On his promotion to London manager, Schloss asked to be allowed to invest his savings, about £100, in the new company.

'I was so pleased at getting his £100,' wrote Bettmann in his memoir notes, 'that I offered him a directorship. Schulte agreed but, at the same time, warned me not to be so lavish, in future, in scattering directorships around.'

Nevertheless, shortage of capital was hampering growth and, in raising resources to £2,000, two more directors were appointed. They were Alderman Tomson and a much-respected Coventry financier, Alfred Friedlander who, like Tomson, had his roots in the ribbon trade. It seems, too, that the quarrel with George Sawyer had been patched up, for he was now chairman.

By now, also, the business had been registered as a limited-liability company and, consequently, the title had become the Triumph Cycle Co Ltd, but it was still a minnow among the whales by comparison with such firms as Singer, which had gone public with the, then, enormous capital of £800,000. However, Triumph were about to get bigger and bolder.

The progress of the bicycle and the pneumatic tyre bore a close relationship, and it was not surprising that Dunlop should have kept an eye on Triumph. One day Bettmann received a summons to Dublin, there to meet Harvey du Cros. A Dubliner, du Cros was the man who had provided financial backing for John Boyd Dunlop; now he told Bettmann that he foresaw a bright future for Triumph and that the Dunlop company was prepared to invest a substantial amount of money in his firm.

Du Cros sent his accountants to inspect the the Triumph books. Finding everything highly satisfactory, they made a favourable report. In consequence, the Triumph Cycle Co Ltd was again reconstituted, this time with a capital of £45,000, of which half was in preference and half in ordinary shares. Bettmann and Schulte were appointed joint managing directors.

A less direct result of the Dunlop involvement was that when John Griffiths, who had been the Dunlop secretary, left to form his own company to wholesale cycles, he took on the agency for Triumph machines. That, in turn, introduced the make to many new retail outlets.

It was becoming obvious that the Much Park Street premises were too small for the growing concern and, in 1907, a move was made to Priory Street. In time, the Priory Street complex was to include buildings on both sides of the road, and to extend to frontages on Dale Street and Cox Street. (Today, much of the site is occupied by Coventry's huge central swimming bath, while other parts lie buried beneath the De Vere Hotel and the new Coventry Cathedral—where, ironically, the Chapel of Industry stands on the site of the old Triumph dispatch bay.)

The Much Park Street works were not, however, abandoned. They became the nominal headquarters of Triumph's secondary business, the Gloria Cycle Co. In addition, they housed the sidecar-body shop and, in later years, the motorcycle service department. The premises were demolished in 1970 after serving for some years as the motor cycle service department of the Coventry City Police.

Once more the firm underwent financial restructuring, and now became a public company. Debenture and preference shares (to the value of £40,000 and £50,000 respectively) were underwritten by Dunlop, but there was a mad scramble for the £80,000-worth of ordinary shares. These were subscribed for ten times over, and many of those who got in early made a quick killing by selling at a substantial profit.

While the company as a business organisation

had been growing apace, the technical side had not been neglected. As early as 1897 the first steps were taken on the path to motor-cycle manufacture. Leader here was Mauritz Schulte, who proposed that Triumph should take up the British rights of the German-made Hildebrand and Wolfmuller. A specimen of the machine was brought to Coventry and studied. Schulte himself learned to ride it, and gave a series of demonstrations at Coventry Stadium. But the time for motor cycles had not yet arrived, the partners decided, and nothing further was done.

Later it was Bettmann's turn to think of powered travel, for he began negotiations with Humber for a manufacturing lease on the Beeston Humber motor cycle and tricycle. This time an agreement was indeed drawn up, and a prototype built and exported to Australia, but the scheme fell through.

Not until 1902 did Triumph at last add a motor cycle to their range, but before then there had been a jolt for the directors. The annual accounts which, up to that time, had shown growing profits, indicated a loss of £1,500. Shocked to the core, a group of angry shareholders at the general meeting began to abuse the directors, accusing them of incompetence. But Bettmann was both willing and able to give as good as he got, and it was only when Schulte tugged his sleeve and begged him to sit down that his spate of anger abated.

Without reference to Bettmann or Schulte the other directors, led by Tomson and Friedlander, made an approach to instrument-manufacturer John Rotherham, asking him to serve on the Triumph board as an additional director. He declined, but promised to act as a sort of financial overseer. After a year he reported that his position was superfluous, as he had found the company's affairs to be in good hands.

Perhaps it was the example set by Alderman Tomson that encouraged Bettmann to become involved in Coventry's civic matters but, by 1907, he was a Liberal member of the city council, and his political activities culminated in his election, in 1913, as Mayor of Coventry. He was still in the mayoral chair when war came in 1914—a remarkable situation for a native of what was, then, an enemy country.

Triumph was not his only interest for he had become, also, chairman of the Standard Motor Co but, because of wartime hysteria, he relinquished that position. In later life his sympathies moved away from Liberalism towards Labour, and he became a close friend of Ramsay MacDonald.

With the outbreak of war there appeared on the scene another man who was destined to have a big say in the shaping of Triumph fortunes. He was Claude V. Holbrook, a staff captain with the purchasing branch of the War Office.

One Sunday morning, with the war but a few weeks old, the telephone rang in Bettmann's home. Could Triumph, asked Captain Holbrook, pack and ship to France, urgently, 100 motor cycles for the British Expeditionary Force? Bettmann promised to do the best he could and set out for the home of his works manager, Charles Hathaway. In turn, Hathaway rounded up as many Triumph workers as he could find, opened up the Priory Street plant, and got the job under way.

That evening the machines were en route for France, the first of over 30,000 Triumphs to be supplied to the allied forces during the four years of war. In that time Holbrook became a frequent visitor to the factory; his capabilities so impressed Bettmann that he resolved to ask him to join the company when peace returned.

Unhappily, the personal relationship between Bettmann and Schulte had been deteriorating; so much so that the two Triumph founders were barely on speaking terms by 1919, and it was Bettmann who induced the board to ask for Schulte's resignation (though there was a golden handshake of £15,000, a small fortune by the standards of the day).

Holbrook, by then a Lieutenant-Colonel (later to become Colonel Sir Claude V. Holbrook), was brought in as the new general manager and, for a time, everything went well. But one point on which Bettmann and Schulte had fallen out concerned bicycle manufacture, on which Triumph had been founded. Bicycles, said Schulte, had served their purpose and should be dropped in favour of car-making. Now, it seemed, Holbrook was of similar mind.

Harry (later, Sir Henry) Ricardo had been commissioned to design and develop a sports motor cycle engine—the famous four-valve Riccy, introduced for the 1922 season. Triumph asked him for a car engine also, and it was this unit, a simple 1,393 cc side-valve, that powered the first production Triumph car. Launched in 1923, it had a top speed of 47 mph and a fuel consumption of 35 mpg.

But Priory Street, with some buildings that rose to seven storeys, was a far-from-ideal location for car manufacture, and this factor must have been partly responsible for the company's subsequent troubles. However, though some sections of car production remained at Priory Street, the situation was eased when the former Dawson car works in Clay Lane was acquired as an assembly plant.

To market the cars, a subsidiary concern, the

Triumph Motor Co Ltd, was formed, while the two-wheelers continued under the wing of the parent Triumph Cycle Co Ltd. The Triumph Cycle name survived until December 1934 (when it was changed to Triumph Co Ltd) though, in fact, the cycle side had been disposed of two years earlier to Associated Cycles (formerly Coventry Bicycles, builders of the big-twin Coventry-B & D and the Villiers-powered Three Spires). Eventually, the bicycle business passed to Raleigh.

The depression of the early 1930s hit Triumph hard. The firm was forced to liquidate various assets and investments in an effort to keep going. Yet, though the motor-cycle side was doing its best to hold prices down (the ultimate was a 98 cc Villiers-engined lightweight, at £16 16s the cheapest Triumph of all time but offered, in 1933, under the Gloria label), the car people went to the opposite extreme.

Incredibly, they chose to press ahead with the luxury, 2,300 cc straight-eight Triumph Gloria Dolomite. In reality this was a Coventry-built copy of the Alfa Romeo Mk 8C for which, in return, Alfa Romeo would have Italian manufacturing rights to the Page-designed 6/1 650 cc Triumph vertical-twin motor cycle engine. Alfa were too busy with aero-engine work to take up this interesting proposal, but Triumph did build three prototype Gloria Dolomites in the Priory Street toolroom.

Donald Healey drove one of them in the 1935 Monte Carlo Rally—at least, he started but wrote off the car when he tried to get the better of a train at a level crossing in Denmark. The car never did get into production, partly because Lloyds Bank had stepped in to safeguard their interests, and Bettmann was demoted from managing director to vice-chairman. The new manager, named Graham, was a Lloyds Bank nominee, and when the expected upturn in fortunes failed to take place it was decided to stop motor cycle production, sell off the Priory Street plant and concentrate all the company's resources on the manufacture of cars at new works that had been acquired in Foleshill Road, Coventry (now occupied by the Dunlop Rim and Wheel Co).

News of these proposals soon reached the ears of Jack Sangster who, in 1932, had personally taken over the Ariel motor cycle business when the original concern was in financial difficulties as the result of a worldwide slump. He had turned it into a very successful enterprise under the name, at first, of Ariel Works (JS) Ltd.

Now, Sangster made contact with Graham and, during a two-hour railway journey from Birmingham to London, they negotiated a deal in which it was agreed that Sangster would purchase the nominal share capital of the Triumph Engineering Co Ltd, already in existence as a non-trading subsidiary of the Triumph Co. After he had provided the engineering company with the necessary finance, that concern would then purchase the stock-in-trade and goodwill of Triumph's motor-cycle business.

As part of the deal, the Triumph Engineering Co would be granted a short-term lease of the whole of the Priory Street premises, together with the motor cycle plant and machinery. In addition, there was an option (subsequently exercised) to buy a substantial part of the old works, plus the machinery and equipment needed for production. The agreement covering the transaction was signed on January 22 1936, and from that date Triumph motor cycles and Triumph cars went their independent ways.

The first move made by Sangster after he had acquired the Triumph Engineering Co Ltd was to invite Siegfried Bettmann, founder of the Triumph name, to become chairman. The invitation, gladly accepted, was an astute move for it provided a strong link with the past successful history of Triumph. Bettmann was held in high regard, not only by the numerous suppliers but also by the distributors and dealers both at home and in the export field. In addition, and most importantly, the many hundreds of Triumph employees engaged in motor cycle manufacture had their morale boosted overnight.

Bettmann, who was then well into his seventies, remained chairman for only a short period—but long enough to have the satisfaction of seeing the new company safely launched on its way to what was, during the subsequent 25 years, probably the most successful era ever enjoyed by any manufacturer in the British motor cycle industry.

Chapter 2

Under new management

IN THE LAST official announcement concerning two-wheelers ever issued by the old Triumph company, in mid-January of 1936, a salute was made to the incoming party.

'The new company,' the statement read, 'will be controlled and managed by men who are motor-cycle specialists, and who have already success-fully demonstrated their ability in the manufac-turing and commercial sides of the industry. Consequently we have no hesitation in expressing the opinion that the business will be carried on vigorously and successfully.

'It is necessary to emphasise that although motor cycles will continue to be marketed under the Triumph name, the company manufacturing them will not be connected with this company (the Triumph Co Ltd) either financially or in any other way.'

Men who were motor cycle specialists? The Sangster family (Charles at first, followed by his son, Jack) had been in control of Ariel fortunes since the mid-1890s. Immediately on leaving the British Army towards the end of the First World War, Jack Sangster conceived the idea of a 'motor cycle on four wheels'. Prototypes embodying a 1,000 cc flat-twin, air-cooled engine were produced at a factory in Tyseley, Birmingham, which at that time belonged to Charles Sangster.

Coventry's long-established Rover Co became interested in the project, and bought not only the design but also the Tyseley factory, with Jack join-ing Rover to help in development and production of what was to become known as the Rover Eight. Production built up rapidly to 350 per week, the largest output of any British car maker of the time.

It was not long before young Sangster (always called Mr Jack by the employees) rejoined his father at Selly Oak, to produce the pert little Ariel Nine light car. Unluckily, its introduction was more or less coincidental with that of the Austin Seven and, after a small number of Nines had been made, Ariel withdrew from the car field.

Selly Oak's resources and energies were switched to motor cycles, the services of Val Page as chief designer were secured, and output was boosted from 50 to 500 Ariel motor cycles a week.

It is necessary to glance at Ariel history for a little while longer before returning to the Triumph

story proper, for in 1928 Edward Turner joined Selly Oak to design and develop that brilliant piece of engineering, the Square Four. However, troubled times lay ahead and, when (as mentioned in the previous chapter) the Ariel Co was reconstituted in 1932, Val Page left to join the Triumph Co, while Edward Turner stayed with Ariel as chief designer.

By that time, Jack Sangster could properly be described as a motor-cycle specialist. The energy and commercial skill which he displayed in rebuild-ing Ariel after the slump of 1932 brought him the unstinted admiration of the entire industry.

To some degree, Sangster's nomination of Edward Turner to double as chief designer and general manager of the Triumph Engineering Co was unexpected. Chief designer, certainly; Turner had already displayed his flair for original thought in the 350 cc ohc Turner of 1927, and in the Ariel Square Four. As yet, though, his managerial qualities were untried.

Another surprise choice was that of C.W.F. Parker as company secretary (a post which he was to retain right through to the 1970s). To the general public, Charles Parker was a journalist and road-tester on the Birmingham staff of *Motor Cycling*, but in truth he was a trained accountant who had joined that magazine because of his enthusiasm for motor cycles.

The new company was lucky, also, in being able to retain Harry Camwell as works manager. He had worked for the old company in a similar cap-acity for many years and was responsible for the smooth transition and the disentangling of the motor-cycle manufacturing facilities from the non-motor-cycle elements—no easy task. To him, also, belongs the credit for the superb quality of Triumph products during his period of office.

On the surface, all seemed placid as the incoming management took up the reins. Up to and including the Val Page 650 cc twin, the nine-model range dis-played at Olympia the previous autumn would be continued in its entirety (the announcement was made at a luncheon for 150 main dealers) and no range alterations were contemplated for some time to come. But there was to be an immediate price rise on the loss-making 250 and 350 cc models.

That was understandable. Motor cycle sales manager under the old company, Harry Perrey was to recall many years later: 'The takeover came at a time when we were stocking up for the spring sales boom. Our dispatch department was chock-full of bikes ready to be sent out, and there were still more machines on the assembly line.'

Harry, personally, was due for a shock. Turner had studied the existing Triumph sales organisation and, in one of his first managerial moves, he decreed that sales should henceforth be conducted out on the road rather than from a central office. The sales manager's position, as such, was abolished and, instead, the country was divided into three sales areas with a manager for each. Perrey was allotted a segment with its apex at Coventry but extending outwards to Cornwall and Wales. Jack Welton, who had been Harry's assistant, was retained at Priory Road to correlate the paperwork of the three area managers.

Nor was that all. The wages bill was too high, it was decided, and the staff were given the option of leaving—or of staying on, at less money. Even though the wage cuts were not too severe, the fact that employees accepted them was, in itself, a sign of the times.

With all possible speed the motor-cycle manufacturing facilities were concentrated in that part of the works which lay on the right-hand side of Priory Street (as seen from Jordan Well). The option to buy was exercised and new office accommodation was then built in what had been the competition and development section at the Dale Street end of the complex. Eventually, the registered address of Triumph was changed, officially, to Dale Street.

The part of the old works on the left of Priory Street remained the property of the old Triumph Co and subsequently passed into the hands of Coventry Corporation. Plans for rebuilding that area of the city had already been drawn up but, before the corporation's demolition squad could get to work, war was declared.

The reshuffle also embraced the transfer into the main plant of the service department that had been located in Much Park Street. Triumph thereby at last gave up their original Coventry home.

By mid-April there was a sign to the public that something was under way, by the announcement of three additions to the range. These were 250, 350 and 500 cc overhead-valve singles named—respectively, and most attractively—the Tigers 70, 80 and 90. Mechanically, the newcomers were derived from the Val Page-designed Mark 5 models, but a hint of Edward Turner's flair for styling was seen in the provision of chromium-plated fuel tanks with top and side panels of silver-sheen, and chromium-plated headlamp shells.

The Tiger specification called for polished cylinder-head ports, stronger valve springs, polished flywheel rims (to reduce oil drag), and 'new-type cast-iron cylinders, hardened and oil-tempered to prolong life and improve friction surfaces'.

Nevertheless these were only interim models and considerable changes were seen in the 11-model range announced for 1937. This impressive list was based on two types of frame, and on the standardisation of a new four-speed, foot-change gearbox, but it encompassed side-valve and overhead-valve singles from 250 to 600 cc. Heading the parade were the three Tiger models, sleeker than when first announced and now graced by high-level exhausts and more pleasingly contoured tanks.

'Three Tigers, three golds' had been the claim when, in September 1936, Ted Thacker (Tiger 70), Allan Jefferies (Tiger 80) and Fred Povey (Tiger 90) completed the International Six Days Trial with a trio of clean sheets to win one of the four manufacturers' team awards earned that year. As a result, three of the 1937 newcomers were pukka trials models for the first time, complete with wide-ratio gearboxes, crankcase undershields, stronger fork springs, and increased ground and mudguard clearances.

They came in all three Tiger capacities and, in celebration, Allan Jefferies took a three-fifty model into runner-up spot in both the Colmore and Bemrose trials. Converting another Tiger 80 to scrambles trim and fitting a high-compression piston, Ken Haynes won the Hants Grand National.

Yet another Tiger 80 was chosen, the same year, by Brooklands tuner and racing man Freddie Clarke, to set the all-time 350 cc Brooklands lap record at 105.97 mph. Clarke's model was a dope-burner, but his tuning ability had not gone unnoticed and he was recruited as head of the Coventry firm's engine-development section.

Not that Edward Turner was impressed with the road-racing scene. 'I am often asked,' he said, 'why Triumph don't show interest in the TT races. The answer is that racing is no longer an attractive proposition for manufacturers. In 1926 or 1927 the position was different, because at least 60 per cent of a racing machine was then based on the standard model. Today, racing machines are special from wheel to wheel, and there is nothing that can be translated into production.

'I don't say that the TT should be abolished, but there should be stock-machine races, and for our part we would be prepared to support such events. I believe other makers would do so, too.'

In the years ahead there were, indeed, production-machine races; and, moreover, Triumphs were to

1: *To celebrate the Queen's Silver Jubilee in 1977, a limited edition of Bonneville 750 cc twins, patriotically finished in silver, with blue panels and red-and-white striping, was announced in July of that year, the first product of Meriden Motor Cycles Ltd after operating independently of NVT.*

2: *Triumph's first: introduced in 1902, this model was essentially a pedal cycle with the Belgian 1¾ hp (239 cc) Minerva engine mounted on the front down tube and driving the rear wheel by belt. Inlet valve was automatically opened by engine suction, the exhaust mechanically operated — and fitted with a manual lifter.*

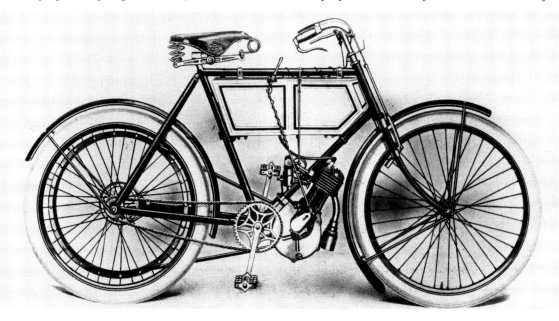

3: (*Above left*) *Mauritz Schulte, the engineer who joined Siegfried Bettmann in 1887, on a 3½ hp Triumph in 1911.*

4: (*Above*) *Siegfried Bettmann in his mayoral robes. He was Mayor of Coventry, 1913-14.*

5: (*Far left*) *Jack Y. Sangster, who took over the motor-cycle side of the Triumph company in 1936. As the Triumph Engineering Co Ltd it became Britain's most renowned motor-cycle producer.*

6: (*Left*) *Edward Turner, switched from Ariel by Jack Sangster in 1936 to become chief designer and general manager of Triumph. His Speed Twin in 1937 set the vogue for parallel-twin engines.*

7: (*Above*) *When the Triumph Engineering Ço Ltd went into business in 1936 with Jack Sangster at the helm, many of the earlier models in updated form were continued. This is the 500 cc Tiger 90 of 1938, a sturdy roadster with a top speed of over 90 mph.*

8: *The first Triumph scooter, the Tigress, with 250 cc twin-cylinder ohv engine, introduced in November 1958.*

9: *An unexploded bomb in the frame shop of the Priory Street, Coventry, works in April 1941 — the second time in the Second World War the factory was smashed in German raids.*

10: *First Speed Twin, announced in July 1937. It was an instant success and its neat, 500 cc, ohv, parallel-twin engine was to become the world's most famous unit. It was to set Triumph on the road to an all-twin range in later years.*

11: *The 350 cc Twenty-One (1964 version). This model, first listed in 1957 as a civilised tourer, was named to mark 21 successful years of the Triumph Engineering Co Ltd; at that time enclosure panels appeared only on the Twenty-One, but were to be adopted for other models later on.*

12: *Triumph tester and consistently successful racing man, Percy Tait forcing one of the Trident three-cylinder models. In production-racing and Formula 750 trim, the Trident has notched many top placings in Europe and America.*

13: *Trident in standard roadster form, as introduced in 1969 with four-speed gearbox and drum brakes, twin-leading-shoe for the front wheel.*

14: *The Trident three-cylinder engine. Cylinder head and valve gear owe much to the design features of the earlier twin-cylinder engines. The alternator is housed below the contact breaker unit in the timing chest.*

15: (*Above*) *Bonneville Salt Flats, Utah, USA: the projectile housing a 650 cc Triumph engine with which Texan Johnny Allen achieved 214.4 mph in September 1956. This world-record claim was never ratified by the FIM. Left to right, designer Stormy Mangham, Johnny Allen, and tuner Jack Wilson.*

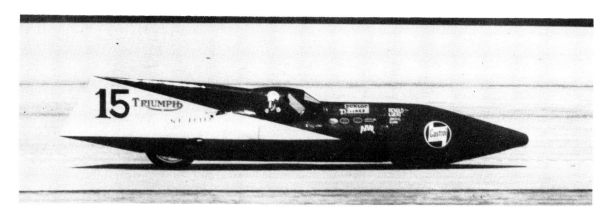

16: (*Above*) *Also at Bonneville, American Bill Johnson sets the official world-fastest record at 224.57 mph in September 1962. His machine, too, was fitted with a Triumph 650 cc twin engine. This record still stands (1975).*

17: (*Left*) *The installation of the two 650 cc Triumph engines in Bob Leppan's Gyronaut X-1 for his record attempts in 1966.*

18: *Gyronaut X-1, which achieved 245.6 mph at Bonneville in August 1966. The 1,300 cc power plant (two Triumph six-fifties) was too large for the speed to rank as an FIM-recognised record. Behind the machine are, left to right, Earl Flanders (referee, American Motorcycle Association), rider Bob Leppan, designer Alex Tremulis, and engineer Jim Bruflodt.*

19: *Johnny Allen.*

20: *Bill Johnson.*

21: *Bob Leppan.*

22: *John Hobbs with his supercharged 1,000 cc Olympus II sets the rear tyre smoking on getaway at the Santa Pod sprint strip.*

23: *Fred Cooper's Cyclotron sprinter with the Shorrock supercharger mounted between the two twin-cylinder engines. To give symmetrical induction plumbing, the rear cylinder head is reversed.*

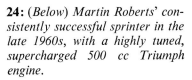

24: *(Below) Martin Roberts' consistently successful sprinter in the late 1960s, with a highly tuned, supercharged 500 cc Triumph engine.*

win them again and again. But a war was to lie between.

A bombshell in another sense had been delivered with the announcement at the end of July 1937 of the Turner-designed Speed Twin, the machine that was to change the thinking of the whole motorcycling world. It had been laid out on the drawing board, claimed Turner, with a maximum speed of 90 mph as the aim. And when the first, hand-made prototype was timed over a measured stretch of road, 90 was just what it did.

In 1938 (and with the benefit of an extra year's development) the sportier Tiger 100 was added. It marked the start of a policy that Turner was to follow for many years: the soft-tuned tourer followed, later, by a zippier companion. Looking well ahead the 350 cc 3TA would be partnered by a Tiger 90 (the old name revived); the 650 cc Thunderbird would have a Tiger 110 counterpart; and even the utility 200 cc (single-cylinder, overhead-valve) Tiger Cub would be followed later by friskier derivatives.

Chapter 3

The Blitz and after

ACROSS THE TOP of the familiar blue covers being made ready for *Motor Cycle's* issue of September 8 1939 ran the exciting promise of a New British 350 cc Twin. Yet the promise was to be delayed, just a little—by six weary years, in fact. A phone call brought the press to a halt, already printed covers were scrapped, and when the press restarted the headline had been changed to the rather duller Modern Fork Design Analysed.

The explanation is that, in that week's issue, Triumph were to have announced their 1940 programme, which included a 349 cc twin, the 3T. This was no mere scaled-down edition of the Speed Twin, but a new design featuring such novelties as rocker boxes integral with the cast-iron cylinder head, and a built-up crankshaft in which the mainshafts were clamped into, instead of being bolted to, the central flywheel.

But, that very week, Hitler had marched his troops into Poland and, in consequence, Britain found herself at war with Germany. So the 3T was shelved. The more immediate need was the rapid equipping of the British Army with motor cycles, and War Department purchasing officers made the rounds of dealers' showrooms, selecting suitable (and quite a few totally unsuitable) models for immediate impressing into military service.

They visited the Triumph works, too, to impound a batch of machines awaiting dispatch, but as the country settled down to a period of inactivity on the military front—the so-called Phoney War—so the War Department rationalised its requirements. Motor cycle mainstays of the British Army at this time were the Norton 16H and BSA M20; to these, Triumph now added the 350 cc 3SW and 500 cc 5SW, the side-valve sloggers of the 1939 civilian range, but dressed in khaki and with an austerity finish.

However, Edward Turner felt that something lighter and more agile was required for modern military duty. Accordingly, he used the postponed 3T engine as the basis of a suggested Army light-weight; the engine was in unit with a three-speed gearbox, and lighting was supplied from the first-ever alternator to be seen on a powered vehicle.

Prototypes were submitted for Army evaluation and, at last, the 3TW was passed for production. A pilot batch of 50 machines was put in hand and, of these, some had been completed and were awaiting dispatch, while others were in a near-complete state on the assembly line, when the Triumph day-shift clocked off and headed homeward through the cold, clear evening of November 14 1940.

At that same moment, on the airfields of Germany, the Luftwaffe was preparing for the first saturation raid of the war. Soon, the sirens shrieked out across the Coventry rooftops as a force estimated at 400 planes approached from the east. Then down hurtled 500 tons of high explosives and 30,000 incendiaries, to rip apart the compact area that was the city's heart.

The Priory Street premises were located within 200 yards of the cathedral, the focal point of the attack, and no factory suffered more than Triumph's.

All 120 employees on the night shift took to the air-raid shelters when the sirens wailed. The shelters were remarkably effective; although high-explosive bombs fell within yards of them, no lives were lost. The sole casualty of any consequence was one man who damaged an ankle when he fell over in the darkness!

As dawn broke the following morning, the works were seen to be a smoking, shattered wreck. Said an eye-witness: 'Although it was more or less possible to walk or crawl around, one was faced on all sides with an impenetrable jungle of rubble mixed with half-melted and twisted iron and steel; what looked like a complete motor cycle could be seen high in the tangle of the roof girders. It was a heart-breaking sight.'

The whole of the factory, including the new offices which had been built only a year earlier, was obviously out of action for an indefinite period. The immediate problem facing Jack Sangster was how and where to hold together the key personnel and retain some semblance of an organisation.

The solution was the taking over of a disused cement-mixer factory at Warwick—home of the Benford Mortar Mixer Co. Temporary offices, stores and workshops were set up; everything that could be salvaged from the wreckage of Priory Street, including machine tools and components, was transferred to the new headquarters. Even the drawing office staggered back into business with the aid of such drawings as could be found in the wreckage.

At the same time the management were considering the longer-term future. They decided in favour of rebuilding the old factory. The foundations and services were still more or less intact, and the factory layout was efficient for motor cycle production. Patently, production could be re-started earlier this way as against the alternative of building a new factory on a virgin site.

Another important attraction of the Coventry site was that a high proportion of the employees lived conveniently near.

But it was not to be. The War Damage Com-

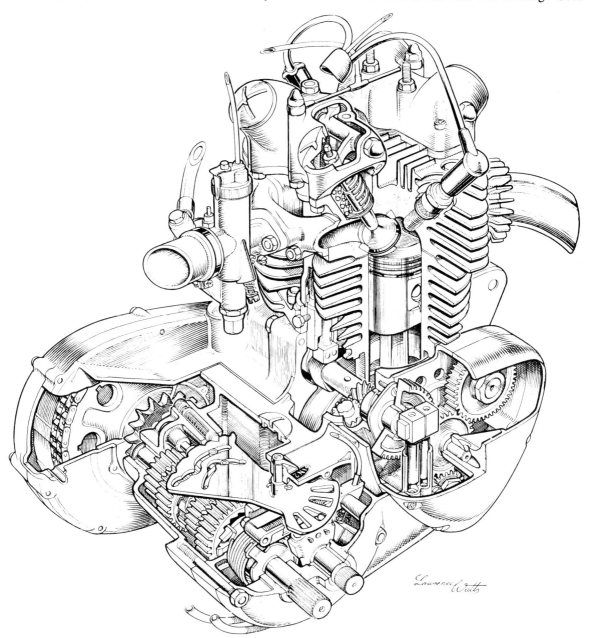

Introduced in 1957 and named the Twenty-One in celebration of the Triumph Engineering Co's coming of age, the 350 cc 3TA was the first of the post-war designs to feature unit construction of engine and gearbox. The engine was extraordinarily neat and compact. The machine was, also, the first Triumph to have partial enclosure of the rear wheel.

mission considered that the Priory Street area would be too vulnerable to further air-raid damage; moreover, the Coventry council had other uses in mind for the long-term development of the city centre.

Eventually, what is now known as the Meriden site was chosen as the most suitable one available. It was an open field located some four miles outside Coventry on what was then the main Coventry–Birmingham road, between the villages of Allesley and Meriden.

The architects immediately set to work on plans for the 'ideal' motor cycle factory, though a major obstacle had still to be overcome. The Meriden Rural District Council refused to give building permission on the grounds that the area was not zoned for industrial purposes—this while a world war raged! Fortunately, at the public hearing of an appeal, the council's objections were overruled by Whitehall.

Construction work went ahead and the new factory was completed at remarkably high speed compared with the time it would take nowadays.

Earlier, the sketchy organisation at Warwick had been strengthened as far as possible and, in spite of more bombing in April 1941, a few of the lesser-damaged shops at Priory Street were reconstructed on a makeshift basis so that small-scale production had restarted there before the move to the new factory in May 1942.

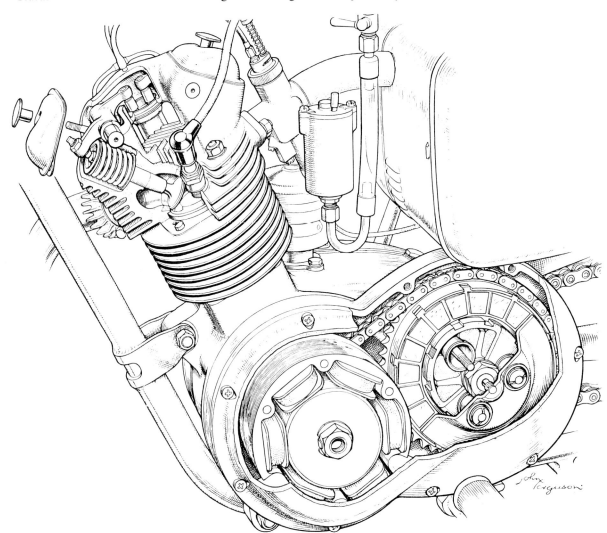

A radical departure from the Triumph twin-cylinder policy, the 150 cc Terrier appeared in 1953. Its engine was straightforward in design and cheap to produce; an alternating-current generator was mounted in the primary chaincase, with the rotor on the engine mainshaft.

A large number of the workforce—women and men—who had been employed in Coventry loyally rejoined the firm, and production got going with a swing at Meriden.

The machine they got busy on was not the 3TW twin. Because of the need for maximum output with the facilities and materials available, a simple, 350 cc overhead-valve single was selected. This was the 3HW, in essence the pre-war 3H but with a redesigned cylinder head and rocker gear.

Incidentally, three of the stillborn 3TW models were salvaged and restored; one of them is now in the National Motor Museum at Beaulieu, Hants.

While Triumph were operating at Warwick differences arose between Edward Turner and his colleagues, with the result that Turner left. Like many other geniuses, Turner was temperamental and difficult to work with, particularly at that time when he was noticeably upset by the Blitz.

However, after a spell of about two years with BSA, he rejoined Triumph and remained managing director until his retirement in the early 1960s.

As Meriden got into its stride, so production of the WD 3HW single was stepped up and now, with extra capacity available, the 500 cc twin made its reappearance—not in a motor cycle frame, but as the power unit of a generator set.

For the Army, a shorn version of the Speed Twin engine was coupled to a six-kilowatt generator to form the GGS (Ground Generating Set). For the Royal Air Force, there came a rather more interesting proposition; they required a light yet powerful set to charge the batteries of the Lancaster bomber while in flight, and the outcome was the AAPP (officially, Airborne Auxiliary Power Plant, but to Triumph workers it was the 'A-squared, P-squared').

To cut weight, the cylinder block and head of the AAPP were cast in silicon-aluminium alloy. That light-alloy top half had an important part to play in Triumph's post-war story for, grafted on to a Tiger 100 crankcase assembly, it took Irish farmer Ernie Lyons to victory in the first post-war Senior Manx Grand Prix of 1946. From the Lyons model there evolved the Triumph Grand Prix racer.

The immediate post-war civilian programme was announced on March 1 1945. It comprised the straightforward 3H single (the WD model, but with polished timing cover and gearbox castings, chromium-plated exhaust pipe, and a black finish with white lining), plus the 500 cc Speed Twin and Tiger 100 and, at long last, the 350 cc 3T. A fourth twin, the Tiger 85, was a sportier version of the 3T, but very few examples of this machine were actually manufactured.

For all four twins there was a hydraulically damped telescopic front fork, but in most other respects they were continuations of the pre-war models. However, the Tiger 100 was not quite the model it had been in 1939. Quoted brake horse-power was dropped from 34 at 7,000 rpm to 30 at 6,500 rpm (the infamous 72-octane pool petrol was mainly to blame), and no longer was an individual dynamometer test certificate issued with each machine.

Of course, in the dark days of wartime it had been difficult to predict just what kind of a post-war market there would be for the motor-cycle industry. Edward Turner had gazed into his crystal ball to see a country hungry for personal transport but without the money for the luxury models of the past. Something cheap to build and cheap to buy was needed, he thought; it would be modest in its performance, but with extensive weather protection in order that the city-gent type of customer could ride to the office without dirtying his respectable suit. The machine of his dream reached prototype form as the 3TU, a light three-fifty twin incorporating a number of ingenious features, but it failed to reach the production stage.

The principal reason for the eclipse of the 3TU was that from the USA had come the cry for big machines. The Americans wanted power and plenty of it, and a modest three-fifty was not for them.

There was, indeed, a market for a city-gent motor cycle, but this was, in the years ahead, to be filled by Lambretta and Vespa scooters. Even with the expanded capacity now available at Meriden, Triumph were unable to build every kind of machine at once.

They went, therefore, for a 650 cc twin, the 71×82 mm Thunderbird which was destined to be just as much of a trendsetter as had been the original Speed Twin. The 500 cc Tiger 100 adopted a light-alloy cylinder block and head. And, from the machines which took Britain's International Six Days Trial squad to victory in 1948, there evolved the 500 cc Trophy TR5—a bike which could go anywhere and do anything.

Following Turner's dictum of a roadster then, after a year's shakedown, a sports version, the 650 cc Tiger 110 came into the range, and it seemed that Meriden were now firmly wedded to the idea of twins. So the announcement of the neat little 150 cc Terrier (later developed into the 199 cc Tiger Cub) came as something of a shock.

Unit-construction and partial rear-wheel enclosure made an appearance with the 3TA of 1957 (named the Twenty-One, in celebration of the

Triumph Engineering Co's coming-of-age). By introducing 175 cc two-stroke and 250 cc four-stroke twin Tigress models, Triumph entered the scooter field. With the addition of the 650 cc twin-carburettor Bonneville, named in appreciation of the exploits of Triumph-riding Americans on the famed Utah Salt Flats, Meriden was riding high.

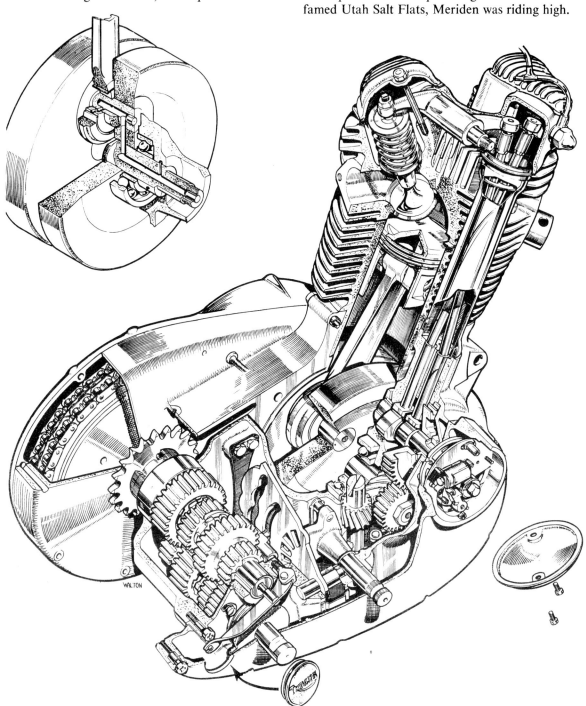

Derived from the 150 cc Terrier, the 200 cc Tiger Cub was a much more robust unit and enjoyed far greater success than its predecessor. The sketch of the flywheel assembly shows the oil feed to the plain-bearing big end —an unusual feature on a high-output, single-cylinder engine.

Chapter 4

The BSA years

THERE IS such a thing as being too successful. By 1950, even with the Meriden plant operating flat out, demand for machines — especially from the United States — was outstripping supplies. Hence the decision was taken to expand the factory so that, by the end of 1951, there would be room for a 15-per-cent increase in output.

The US sales were largely the result of vigorous promotion efforts by Johnson Motors Inc of Pasadena, California, whose association with Triumph started in the summer of 1939 when Edward Turner was sent to the States by Jack Sangster as therapeutic treatment after Turner lost his wife in a car crash near their home on the Coventry – Kenilworth road.

As related in Chapter 11, up to 1950 Johnson Motors was the sole distributor for the whole of the US but, despite the firm's splendid performance, it became obvious that it was not possible to cover the eastern part of that vast country from California. Efforts to find a suitable distributor in the east failed and Triumph set up its own organisation there, the Triumph Corporation. It started operations at Baltimore, Maryland, in January 1951, and was remarkably successful, working in harmony with Johnson Motors, which remained an independent entity owned by Bill Johnson.

Back home at Meriden, the business went from strength to strength, and Jack Sangster was advised that it would be imprudent to continue as a private company because of the penal estate duties that would be levied in the event of his death.

Some years earlier — in December 1944, in fact — when he sold his interest in Ariel to BSA, Sangster had agreed to an undertaking that if he wished, at any future date, to sell Triumph he would give BSA the first refusal. Consequently, talks were started and, ultimately, the Triumph motor-cycle business which Sangster had purchased for about £50,000 in 1936 was sold to BSA for little short of £2½ million; and the price did not include the Triumph Corporation of Baltimore, the subject of a later deal. When the contract was signed in March 1951, Triumph had well over £1 million cash in the bank. The business was certainly a plum worth picking!

Jack Sangster became a director of BSA, and was elected chairman in May 1956, following Sir Bernard Docker's removal from the board.

The BSA organisation was nothing short of an industrial empire at that time. It included Daimler, making cars, buses and military vehicles; Hooper, the coachbuilders; BSA Cycles; BSA Machine Tools; BSA Stationary Engines; BSA Guns; BSA Sintered Products; Carbodies; Jessop, producing special steels; and there were various foundries as well. The motor-cycle companies under the BSA umbrella were BSA, Triumph, Ariel, Sunbeam and New Hudson. At this stage, Edward Turner was appointed managing director of the BSA automotive division (which included Daimler, as well as the motor-cycle interests).

News of the link-up was not spread around in banner headlines, and only gradually did the motor-cycling public learn of the merger. It might have been expected that there would now be an integration of the Meriden and Small Heath ranges, but this was not the policy of the management. BSA built 500 and 650 cc twins in standard and sports versions and so, in direct competition, did Triumph. For police duty BSA offered the A10 model; Triumph, the Saint.

There was, however, some co-operation in the scooter field. Small Heath marketed a machine under the Sunbeam name, and Meriden a similar model, except for the colour scheme, as the Triumph Tigress. Both machines were listed with a choice of a 175 cc, single-cylinder, two-stroke engine or a 250 cc, ohv, twin engine. These scooters failed to find much favour with the public, and were soon dropped from the ranges.

Later on, Edward Turner produced the Triumph Tina scooter with automatic, variable gearing by belt and pulleys, but the world-wide scooter market was already on the wane and this venture into scooters was, again, anything but a success.

As the years went by, BSA enthusiasts bought Beesas and Triumph fans had eyes only for the Bonneville and its sisters. (The Bonneville name, incidentally, derived from the speed exploits of Triumph riders in America on the famous Salt Flats at Bonneville, Utah — see Chapter 8.)

But the success story of Triumph motor cycles was was not plain sailing all the way. There were a few disappointments. One instance was the ingenious spring hub. It was introduced (as an extra) for the

1948 season with great hopes that a satisfactory solution had been found to the problem of springing the rear wheel of a motor cycle. By 1954, however, it had to give way to pivoted-fork rear suspension, which was more efficient and easier to service.

Some years later came another instance, with the very attractive partial enclosure offered first on the Twenty-One model and then on others. But after a few years the motor cyclists of the world clearly demonstrated that they preferred their machines naked, with the machinery open to view!

The profits earned by the motor-cycle division were never disclosed to the public, but the Triumph figures, certified by Charles Parker, who was a director and secretary of the Triumph Engineering Co from its inception in 1936 and who played an important role in its success story, make it clear that the firm remained healthy. Average annual profit for the 20 years, 1950 to 1969, was no less than £644,000! This was a magnificent achievement. It has probably never been approached by any other manufacturer in the 75-year history of the British motor-cycle industry.

Although the profits of the motor-cycle side of BSA cannot be pinpointed, the annual reports to shareholders of the whole group showed that total profits, before tax, in 1956 (when Jack Sangster became chairman) were £1,604,000. By 1960, BSA's centenary year, he was able to report an all-time record profit of £3,418,000 as he handed over the chairmanship to Eric Turner (no relation to Edward Turner), who had joined the group as chief executive a year earlier.

By this time, many of the group's less profitable activities had either been sold or closed down. These included BSA Cycles, Hooper and Daimler. The deals brought considerable benefit to the financial strength of the business. Subsequently, Jessop and the whole machine-tool complex were sold. Alfred Herbert, the world-famous machine-tool company, bought the latter, the purchase consideration being in Herbert shares. Unfortunately, they depreciated in value so enormously that, when they were ultimately turned into cash, BSA suffered a loss of several million pounds.

The dynamic and talented Edward Turner continued as managing director of the motor-cycle division until April 1964, when he retired at his own request, though continuing as a non-executive director of the parent group company. He was replaced by Harry Sturgeon, a first-class salesman but, coming from the aircraft industry, he had no experience of the motor-cycle business. He was likeable, energetic and anxious to force the pace; unhappily, he died after a short illness during his third year with the division. Bert Hopwood, who started his career in the Ariel drawing office and, later, designed the Norton and BSA (A10) twins, was second in command to Harry Sturgeon during his short reign.

Sales had been going well and, for their export achievements in the preceding years, BSA and Triumph were both granted the Queen's Award for Industry in 1967 and 1968.

In February 1967 Sturgeon's responsibilities were taken over by Lionel Jofeh. He, too, came from outside the motor-cycle industry and brought ideas for new and very expensive projects. Among them was the setting-up of Umberslade Hall, a country mansion in Warwickshire, as a lavishly equipped research and development centre. Apart from the capital cost, it probably added some £750,000 a year to overhead charges. Nevertheless, world-wide business was brisk, and the expansionist, forward-looking policy being adopted seemed safe enough at the time, particularly to the group of young, high-pressure executives who had joined the organisation.

In the late summer of 1968 the covers were taken off a new model which had been under development for some while — it was the 750 cc three-cylinder Trident (see Chapter 7). Intended to compete in the superbike market, particularly in the US, its specification was lavish and, inevitably, the machine was costly to make. After a few teething troubles had been cleared, the Trident enjoyed reasonably good sales, and put up some sparkling performances in road racing.

The Trident was paralleled in the BSA range by the Rocket 3, in its essentials an almost identical machine. Other than for the unsuccessful scooters mentioned earlier, this was the first time the BSA-Triumph organisation had marketed substantially similar motor cycles under the two names. This change in policy was, perhaps, more significant than it seemed then, bearing in mind the financial troubles ahead, for many of those with wide experience in the motor-cycle field considered the practice fundamentally unwise. Among them is the retired veteran Jack Sangster. He had always argued that it undermines pride of ownership among riders; it is questionable whether two names will sell more of a first-class product; the cost of effective advertising and distribution under the two-name policy is, obviously, very much higher and spare-parts service has to be duplicated, adding to costs.

Meanwhile, in the States, Johnson Motors of California was purchased and rehoused in a new and elaborate, purpose-built headquarters and then, to a large extent, amalgamated with the Triumph Corporation of Baltimore, which had been acquired by the group some years earlier. Denis McCormack, who went to America from England as a young man and who had been chiefly responsible for the growth of the Triumph Corporation since 1951 and who really understood the market, was retired.

Things soon began to go awry, and McCormack was recalled out of retirement for a period to grapple with the problems arising from major errors in gauging the sales probabilities in the States. First the market was underestimated. Next overestimated — and this, combined with very late deliveries, landed the US organisation with huge unsold stocks at the end of the season. They could be cleared only at a big loss.

On the design side a serious error at about this time was the introduction of a new frame common to both BSA and Triumph 650 cc models. Based on a single, large-diameter spine tube serving also as an oil reservoir, it was a good inch too high for riding comfort; prototype testers said so; pressmen who rode pre-production versions said so. But nothing was done about it. The frame went into production and the public gave it the welcome it deserved.

But perhaps the biggest blunder to influence the fortunes of the BSA group and, inevitably, Triumph, was the introduction of the Ariel 3 tricycle moped. It was said that sophisticated market research showed a world-wide demand for such a machine. Production was planned on the basis of 2,000 units a week. In the event, only a few hundred machines were sold in the weeks following an elaborate and expensive launch in May 1970. This flop may well have involved a loss approaching £2 million.

The motor-cycle division was trying to do too much. For instance, the 1971 line-up included no fewer than 13 models (BSA and Triumph) which were entirely new or substantially changed from their predecessors. This programme led to chaos in the factories and never got off the ground. Among the intended newcomers was the Edward Turner-designed, 350 cc, double-overhead-camshaft twin, the Triumph Bandit (BSA Fury). It was prematurely tooled up for production at great cost but, owing to subsequent major development problems, failed to reach the market.

The consequence of these and other misfortunes was a very sharp reduction in profit in 1969 and 1970, followed by disaster in 1971, when the BSA group accounts showed a loss of £8,500,000.

Further big losses followed and led to complete collapse. Lionel Jofeh, managing director of the motor-cycle division, was retired in July 1971, and Eric Turner, chairman of BSA, resigned the following November.

Lord Shawcross, who had been a non-executive director from January 1968, and had a clear appreciation of the group's problems, was requested by the company's bankers and others to take over as chairman. Reluctantly he agreed to serve, and Barclays Bank, supported by the Export Credits Guarantee Department, granted overdraft facilities up to £10 million. A new chief executive, Brian Eustace, was immediately appointed.

Although Lord Shawcross and a reconstructed board of directors made a valiant attempt to restore the fortunes of the group, the year to the end of July 1972 produced another big loss — some £3,300,000. In the months which followed, results were no better. Bankruptcy seemed inevitable unless government help was forthcoming.

Serious discussions now began with the Department of Trade and Industry and, eventually, a scheme was hatched. Its essentials were that a new company, to be called Norton Villiers Triumph, would be formed with a capital of £10,000,000, almost half of which would be subscribed by the government and the remainder by Manganese Bronze Holdings — the parent company of Norton Villiers, manufacturers of Norton machines since 1966 on acquiring the remains of the bankrupt Associated Motor Cycles Ltd. MBH would make a bid for the whole of the BSA organisation (including, of course, Triumph).

Norton Villiers Triumph would then acquire from MBH the Norton Villiers company, and MBH would retain the whole of the non-motor-cycle interests. The effect was to create a combined organisation of the two major British manufacturers with a board of directors and management to concentrate wholly on the motor-cycle business. The NVT brief was to evolve, with the help of this substantial new investment, a sound enterprise capable of competing with the Japanese industry in world markets and of making a profit. This brief — to ensure a viable commercial undertaking — was to have enormous significance in the months ahead.

The scheme was accepted by the BSA shareholders and that was the end, for all practical purposes, of the old-established BSA group, with its Triumph subsidiary, as an independent public company. From the chaos, Norton Villiers Triumph emerged in July 1973.

Chapter 5

The Meriden convulsion

IN THE LONG run-up discussions before the formation of NVT, the Department of Trade and Industry had agreed to what became known as the two-factory plan for the British motor-cycle industry. It meant the closure of the relatively small factory at Meriden, Warwickshire, with Triumph production switched to the BSA works at Small Heath, Birmingham, which, at over 1 million sq ft, was more than three times the size of Meriden.

This seemed to be the only plan to make sense. NVT was not created, with government initiative and a loan, to perpetuate the massive BSA losses unavoidable while both Meriden and Small Heath were operating.

Access to all the BSA group books and records, possible only when NVT was finally set up in July 1973, confirmed the two-factory decision to be right, and the NVT directors formally approved the plan in early September. Losses were continuing at the rate of about £4 million a year, so speedy action was essential. The public announcement of the Meriden closure came on Friday, September 14, shortly after some 80 shop stewards had been informed during a meeting held in the canteen at the works.

This fateful day marked the beginnings of a political storm that was to rage for the next 18 months and repeatedly to lead to television, radio and press news stories during that time.

Some 1,750 people were employed at Meriden. Most of them faced redundancy, with the rundown starting in February 1974. The stewards were invited to discuss the arrangements for an orderly rundown. There was a possibility of delaying the date, but a decision would have to be made promptly so that orders could be placed with outside suppliers of raw materials and components.

The stewards refused to discuss the timetable for the rundown and imposed a 'work-in'. Senior members of the staff were barred from the premises and no completed machines were allowed to be dispatched.

At the dramatic meeting on September 14 Leslie Huckfield, Labour MP for Nuneaton, had been present and at one stage had become the stewards' spokesman at the microphone. He warned Dennis Poore, the NVT chairman, that the closure plan was 'not the way things are done in Coventry' and

that the management had a 'major fight on its hands'. The next week he, with Keith Speed, Conservative MP for Meriden, and Maurice Edelman, Labour MP for Coventry NW, had a meeting with the minister responsible for industrial development at the DTI, Christopher Chataway, who had been the architect of the setting-up of NVT and had first announced the government's plans in the House of Commons on March 19.

The local MPs were reminded that the government's objective in investing nearly £4.9 million in NVT — it was an investment, though free of dividends for three years, not a grant — was to create a competitive and profitable motor-cycle industry under section 8 of the Industry Act. The function of NVT was not to maintain jobs; if it were, the authority for the financial support would have been section 7 of the Act. There was, at that time, no shortage of jobs for engineering workers in the Coventry area.

Denis Johnson had emerged as the leading spokesman for the Meriden shop stewards and becoming prominent, too, in all the publicity, was Bill Lapworth, Coventry district secretary of the Transport and General Workers' Union. Their attitude was epitomised by Denis Johnson early in October: 'It is our factory,' he said, 'and we are not going to let it go without a fight. All we want is a practical solution other than closure.' At about this time, too, the suggestion of the workers forming a co-operative and buying the factory was put forward as a serious proposal during one of the many meetings with NVT management.

The tentative scheme was to finance the purchase partly by the £1 million or so redundancy money the workforce would receive and partly from other sources not clearly disclosed at the time but possibly by contributions from sympathisers.

NVT agreed to give such a co-operative first refusal on the land and buildings and anything else the company intended to sell — obviously the last would not include the tools urgently needed at the Small Heath plant to start production and assembly of the three-cylinder Trident models there. The repercussion at Small Heath of the Meriden stalemate was most serious. Apart from Bonneville components no longer required, engine-gear units and many other major parts for Tridents had formerly been made at Small Heath and transported to Meriden for assembly into Meriden-made frames. Without the tools to make the frames and a few other essentials, work at Small Heath had been brought to complete standstill.

NVT was forced, therefore, to make new drawings and obtain new tools. This took time, cost nearly £500,000 and caused a delay until April 1974 before Trident production could start at Small Heath.

Before that milestone came up, the steady round of meetings had produced no likely breaking of the deadlock and, in consequence, redundancy notices were issued at the end of October. Meriden would close officially on November 10 1973, instead of the planned rundown starting three months later as originally announced.

But paying off the workers with redundancy money solved nothing. They continued the blockade, and round-the-clock picketing ensured that nothing left the factory and no NVT staff got in. The pickets were holding over 2,500 finished and 1,500 or so part-finished machines, worth over £2 million, in the factory, stopping the supply of spares and keeping the machinery idle. Dealers throughout the world could get neither new machines nor spares to keep those on the road going. Some of them, specialising exclusively on Triumph, faced bankruptcy.

By now many of the Meriden men were finding jobs elsewhere, but the hard core were more determined than ever and were succeeding in getting wide coverage on television and in newspapers on what had become a 'human' story. Banners and placards were hung on the factory railings. Demonstrations and marches were arranged. A mock funeral procession was held and a deputation paraded outside the NVT office in London and the House of Commons.

Of course, the pickets were occupying the factory illegally and could have been ordered out by the police. However, with the government having a stake in the new company, the directors were under pressure from the DTI to negotiate rather than apply to the courts for the law to be imposed.

Protracted discussions were held without success. Eventually, the minister invited Mr Poore and another NVT director to attend a meeting with Harry Urwin, deputy secretary of the T&GWU, together with Coventry district officials of the T&GWU and the AUEW.

The meeting was held on November 30 in Mr Chataway's office. The plan proposed by the minister was that work should resume at the factory on the basis of a labour-only contract, already used in the building industry and commonly called 'the lump'. The arrangement would continue until July 1974, the date originally planned by NVT up to which production would carry on. An option would be granted to sell certain assets to the co-operative but, if this had not been exercised by April, an orderly rundown was to be arranged to finish by the July target date. This proposal, which was labelled Plan 5, was accepted in principle by those present, subject to confirmation by the Meriden pickets.

As negotiations proceeded there seemed a chance that this plan could become a reality. But the weeks slipped by as meeting after meeting was held. Some of them lasted all day and many were lit by flickering candles. That winter the miners were on strike, electricity was rationed and factories were working only three days a week to save fuel.

Eventually, by the end of January 1974, a draft agreement was formulated. It was then ratified by the pickets, but the directors of NVT, who had originally welcomed the proposals on the expectation that work would start in early December, were now facing a different situation. So much time had been lost that the expected advantages were much reduced and substantial losses were being incurred because of the three-day working week, no end to which appeared to be in sight. The directors considered that to use the company's dwindling resources to provide the working capital for 'the lump', as required in the proposals, would be an unjustifiable risk and could jeopardise the ability of NVT to finance its affairs long enough to realise its own profitability.

The minister had to be told that, unless the government would supply the working capital, NVT could not ratify the agreement. As further government finance was ruled out, this plan had to be abandoned.

NVT's shortage of working capital was becoming a more serious worry. The company had been formed in the expectation of selling the 2,500 completed machines and spares locked up in Meriden, and of realising on the disposal of the land and buildings. It should have had at least £5 million either in the bank or in the pipeline to it. Furthermore, production of Tridents should have started at Small Heath.

Dennis Poore was sorely tempted, in exasperation with the seemingly endless negotiations, finally to invoke the law. After all, the DTI had confirmed that there was no possibility of public money being provided for the co-operative and it was looking certain that the men could not raise loans through the usual commercial channels.

for any achievement of its own, but as a pawn in political conflict.

Next day, March 6, the setting up of the Meriden workers' co-operative was formally ratified. Mr Benn greeted the completion of the documents as a 'new chapter in the history of the motor-cycle industry'. The new organisation received just under £5 million from the taxpayer and began to trade under the name of the Meriden Motor Cycle Co-operative.

Dennis Poore was rather less effusive than Tony Benn. 'In the atmosphere of euphoria which, naturally, surrounds today's happenings,' he said, 'I must strike a cautious note. This is, of course, an important milestone in the history of the industry and I would not like there to be any doubt about its significance. But I would be less than honest if I allowed it to be thought that we believe this outcome provides a sound, lasting and sensible solution to the industry's problems unless further substantial investment is provided.'

The Meriden blockade was ended. NVT began to remove its property from the factory in a sudden new atmosphere of cordiality. At last the agony appeared over. NVT and, with it, Triumph had survived.

Part of the arrangement for starting the Meriden Co-operative was a manufacturing contract to supply NVT with 750 cc Tigers and Bonnevilles until July 1977. The prices agreed at the beginning were, of course, rapidly overtaken by inflation, but were upped to the satisfaction of both sides until the autumn of 1976. At this point it became impossible for NVT to agree to further large increases, and it seemed an impasse had been reached.

However, after some seven months of intensive negotiations, the Government made a grant of £500,000 with which the Co-op acquired from NVT the Triumph name and the world-wide distributor and dealer franchises, together with quantities of spare parts, most of which were located at NVT's subsidiaries. The severing of the contract, during which NVT had bought some 23,000 machines from the Co-op, seemed to suit both sides.

Now the Co-op was on its own, but still needed more help. The criticisms by senior civil servants that the quality of management did not justify further investment was overcome by the introduction, at the instigation of Harold Lever, Chancellor of the Duchy of Lancaster, of Lord Stokes to advise the Co-op on overseas marketing and Sir Arnold Weinstock's GEC team to advise on the running of the factory and the marketing of the motor cycles at home.

GEC assistance included the purchase of a stock of 2,000 Bonnevilles accumulated by the Co-op during the price negotiations with NVT before money ran out and the factory had been forced into a six-week lay-off. GEC undertook to release the machines when they were required by the market, and was, in effect, providing home-market finance.

Yet the Meriden Co-operative's major weakness remained—it needed resources and technical expertise to design and develop new models.

An opportunity had to be missed in the spring and early summer of 1976 when NVT came up with a plan for the Meriden factory to produce a 900 cc version of the Trident. Much of the development work had already been completed by NVT. The Co-op needed probably no more than about £200,000 to implement this programme but could get no response from the Department of Industry.

In the summer of 1977 a Co-op inspired variant of the Bonneville was introduced: the Silver Jubilee 750 cc model with appropriate red-white-blue paintwork and plenty of chromium plating.

A surprise announcement came in August 1977 when Denis Johnson, a leader of the sit-in who became chairman of the Co-op, decided he would resign to devote his talents elsewhere. John Nelson, one of the Triumph Engineering Co's stalwarts and for some years service manager, who was later with Norton Villiers, became managing director.

Chapter 6

World trendsetter

ON ACQUIRING Triumph in 1936, Jack Sangster switched Edward Turner from Ariel in Birmingham to the Coventry works. Turner set about rationalising the range and injecting a new enthusiasm into the whole Triumph set-up.

For the 1937 range he offered the Tigers 70 (250 cc), 80 (350 cc) and 90 (500 cc) sports, single-cylinder ohv models, all of which made a big impression with their workmanlike technical features and eye-appeal. But, secretly, Turner was devoting most of his time to pushing forward with the machine which was to have more impact on the evolution of motor cycles than any other technical development. The machine was the Model T (its nomenclature when announced in July 1937), very soon to be known as the 500T Speed Twin.

It was an immediate success, and was the inspiration for all the parallel twins that were to come from the drawing boards of other designers for decades afterwards. But for the Second World War, almost every British factory competing in the big-bike market would have listed a similar model within five years. As it was, they came forward with their parallel twins in the late 1940s.

There was nothing whatever new about the parallel-twin concept. It had been considered by technicians from the very early years of the internal-combustion engine. Only four years before Turner announced his 500 cc, overhead-valve Speed Twin, his designer-colleague at Coventry, the illustrious Val Page, had produced his 650 cc, ohv parallel twin for the 1934 range.

Why, then, was Turner's version such an enormous success? Here is his justification for the bold step he had taken: 'A twin gives better torque. It will run at higher revolutions than a single of similar capacity without unduly stressing major components. Because the firing intervals are equal, which means even torque, the low-speed pulling is better. The engine gives faster acceleration, is more durable, is easier to silence and is better cooled. In every way it is a more agreeable engine to handle.' It will be noted that Turner's twin had even firing intervals. Therefore the cranks were at 360 degrees, and balance characteristics were similar to a single's.

But, since these favourable aspects of the Speed Twin were known to all technicians, there was obviously far more to the explanation than that. At the time, Turner may not have been fully alert to influences at work other than technical advantages. The single-cylinder engine had been regarded as the best for motor cycle use for over 30 years; motor cyclists were conservative and had always been sceptical of innovation. Probably, then, because the Speed Twin unit was so neat and looked like a two-port single it was much more readily accepted than, say, a vee-twin or a flat-twin.

In fact, the engine was so close in dimensions and weight to the other ohv five-hundred in the range, the Tiger 90, that the Speed Twin employed the Tiger 90 gearbox, frame, fork, hubs and other components, and came out some 5 lb lighter at 365 lb, fully equipped.

Moreover, the new engine was right from the start. It had no weaknesses that had to be ironed out by further development during early production. True, the six-stud fixing of the cylinder-base flange to the crankcase mouth was quickly changed to an eight-stud arrangement after a few cases of pulling away had cropped up, but this problem was very quickly dealt with, and the change was on the drawing board for the higher-performance Tiger 100 version introduced a year later.

And with his seeming unerring instinct for what would appeal to motor cyclists, Turner had given the Speed Twin a trim, zestful, and attractive image—even the name was just right for the times.

Finally, Turner was already showing his flair for designing with a thought for production costs. His new bike came out at £75, only £5 more than the Tiger 90 despite twice the number of valves, pistons, connecting rods and other components. Most designers of the period were inclined to stress that any multi-cylinder engine was more complicated and certain to be much more expensive to produce than a single.

The relatively small overall width of the twin was achieved by using a single, iron casting for the cylinders and a one-piece, cast-iron cylinder head. This allowed the crankshaft to be narrow, with the flywheel between the cranks, and made a middle bearing for the shaft unnecessary, so keeping the crankcase width to a minimum. In fact, the case was marginally narrower than that of the single-

Edward Turner's world-famous design, the 500 cc Speed Twin, which was announced in July 1937. The six-stud attachment for the cylinder block to the crankcase was changed to a heavier flange with eight studs the following year, but otherwise only minor modifications were introduced over a long period. The Speed Twin set the pattern for multi-cylinder motor cycle engines for more than 40 years.

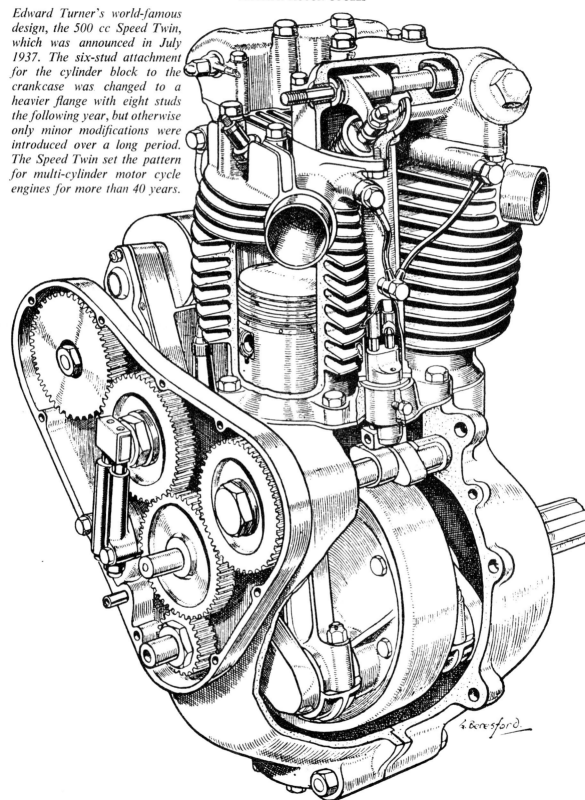

25: *Special supercharged version of the Val Page-designed parallel-twin engine, reduced in capacity for an attempt at Brooklands in 1934 to win* The Motor Cycle *trophy for the first multi-cylinder 500 cc machine to exceed 100 miles in an hour. The trophy was won by New Imperial.*

26: *After the trophy battle was over, the Triumph was used in 1935 by McEvoy as a roadster machine in this form for experimental work on supercharged induction. Most noticeable external change was the long induction pipe surrounding the cylinder head connecting the supercharger with the inlet ports.*

27: (*Above*) *In 1938, Ivan Wicksteed was riding a supercharged Speed Twin at Brooklands. Here he is setting the 500 cc lap record at 118.02 mph in October 1938, nearly 1¾ mph up on the previous record held by Denis Minett on a Norton.*

28: (*Left*) *Upright engines in the bottom-bracket position first appeared in the Triumph programme in 1904. This is the 3 hp model, with the Belgian Fafnir engine.*

29: *First engine to be designed and produced by Triumph, the 'three-horse' of 1905-06. Valves were opened by cams formed internally in the timing gears, with bell-cranks and tappets interposed.*

30: *A two-stroke Triumph, the 225 cc Junior, first marketed for the 1914 season. It had neither clutch nor kick-starter. Operation of the two-speed gear was by cable from a handlebar lever.*

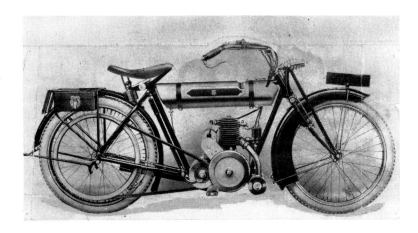

31: *In cloying Flanders mud during the First World War, a German prisoner gives a hand to a British dispatch rider. Note the leather strap just below the horizontal front-fork spring to prevent excessive fork flutter.*

32: *(Below) The ubiquitous 550 cc Model H to military specification in the 1915-18 period. It was fitted with a Sturmey-Archer three-speed gearbox. The cylindrical leather box on the rear-mudguard stay encloses a spare driving belt.*

33: (*Above*) *A step forward in Triumph technical history came in 1919 with the launch of the all-chain-drive Model SD with 550 cc engine. It was fitted with a Triumph gearbox, and a shock absorber was incorporated in the clutch.*

34 and 35: *Shown in prototype form at Olympia, London in late 1922, the 350 cc unit-construction Model LS did not reach the production stage until about a year later after a number of modifications had been made. The large cover plate on the nearside of the crankcase (above) gave easy access to the overhung crank and big-end assembly*

36: *The machine that astonished the British motor-cycle industry, the 1925 Model P with 500 cc engine, three-speed gearbox and all-chain drive for only £42 17s 6d! The contracting band brake for the front wheel was changed in favour of an internal expanding brake after the first 20,000 machines had been made.*

37 and 38: *Superseding the four-valve 500 cc Ricardo super-sports engine, the two-valve Model TT (right) was developed at Brooklands by famous rider-tuner Victor Horsman. The complete Model TT machine (below), as it was marketed in 1927, was outstandingly business-like in appearance.*

39: *First signs of the 'clean look' which threatened to become a fashion in the early 1930s — as did inclined engines. This is the 500 cc Model NT of 1931, with pressed-steel covers concealing crankcase and gearbox.*

40: *More enclosure, seen on the 1932 500 cc Silent Scout, though the panels were listed at extra cost. This particular model justified its name by being one of the quietest machines mechanically and on the exhaust ever produced.*

41: *Simple power unit of Triumph's lightweight for the 1933 season, the 150 cc ohv Model XO was equipped with coil ignition.*

42: *The 500 cc four-valve Ricardo engine of 1921. The two pairs of parallel valves were set at 90 degrees to each other and the design of the cylinder-head casting gave particularly robust support for the rocker mountings. Cylinder finning was shallow, and long bolts, extending to the heavy base of the finning, retained the cylinder head.*

43: *The roadster Ricardo model: it earned a great reputation for good, flexible pulling and sweet running.*

44: *The TT Ricardo machine as used in the 1922 Senior race. Compared with the earlier version, the stroke was reduced and the bore increased to allow bigger valves to be used, and the exhaust ports were splayed instead of being parallel.*

45: *The 6/1 parallel twin announced in 1933. Its 650 cc engine was sturdy and extremely reliable, but the complete machine was heavy. The hand-change gearbox was a disadvantage at a time when positive-stop foot change was the vogue.*

46: *All-gear drive was employed on the 650 cc engine for the camshaft, located in the crankcase to the rear of the cylinder block, and the Lucas Mag-dyno. The push-rods operated through a tunnel in the cylinder casting.*

47: *For comparison — the 500 cc Speed Twin engine that entered the range four years after the 6/1 and began Triumph's run of success in the twin-cylinder field. Although this is the 1952 version, it was similar in its essential features to the original of 1937.*

cylinder Tiger 90, and an identical primary-chain line was possible.

Sturdy, ribbed flanges were part of the single-piece, manganese-molybdenum, alloy-steel stampings forming each crank, bobweight and mainshaft. Bolts clamped the flywheel between the flanges to make up the complete crankshaft assembly, which ran on ball-bearings of $2\frac{3}{4}$ inch overall diameter, one each side.

The connecting rods were forgings in RR56 light alloy, to cut down weight and obtain maximum heat conductivity, and ran directly on the big-end journals. The big-end caps, with their integral bolts, were also in manganese-molybdenum steel, and lined with white metal—a safety precaution, since the white metal would run before more damage was done if a bearing tightened.

Pistons were of orthodox, aluminium-alloy, full-skirt type, each with one slotted scraper and two compression rings. The hollow, taper-bore gudgeon pins were retained by wire circlips and operated in phosphor-bronze bushes in the connecting rods.

Camshafts, exhaust at the front, inlet at the rear, were located in transverse tunnels high in the crankcase castings, and ran in phosphor-bronze bushes. Wide-base tappets operated in cast-iron guides, and duralumin push-rods actuated the forged rockers with phosphor-bronze bushes running on hollow spindles. The light-alloy rocker boxes were each retained by six studs.

Spur gears drove the two camshafts and the Magdyno, and the double plunger pump for the dry-sump lubrication system was located in the timing chest and driven by the inlet camshaft.

The Speed Twin engine produced 26 bhp at around 6,000 rpm, and gave a top speed of over 90 mph, with 74 mph at the end of a quarter-mile from a standing start.

First variant was the Tiger 100, with 8-to-1 (instead of 7.2-to-1) compression ratio given by forged, slipper-pattern pistons, polished internals and improved gas flow through the induction manifold and ports. An aluminium-bronze cylinder head was available at £5 extra on the basic price of £80.

From the Speed Twin stemmed a long line of world-famous parallel-twin machines which retained the essential characteristics of 360-degree cranks with the flywheel between them, high camshafts located fore and aft, a one-piece cylinder casting and one-piece cylinder head. Over a period of nearly 40 years, sizes have gone down to 350 cc and up to 650 and 750 cc. Some engines have had light-alloy cylinders and heads. There have been Tigers, Trophies, Daytonas, Thunderbirds, Bonnevilles and Adventurers among other names, but all owed their basic design and many of their detail features to the original Speed Twin.

Yet in one fundamental characteristic the design had a weakness that was to become more noticeable as, over the years, power outputs were to climb. The balance of a crankshaft with 360-degree throws is precisely similar to that of a single-cylinder shaft. This means it has serious out-of-balance forces which are felt as vibration periods at certain revolutions. On the twins it is a high-frequency vibration that is not only uncomfortable for the rider but can fracture mountings and fittings.

For years this shortcoming was not considered serious enough to outmode the design, but as the demand for bigger engines and more luxury became insistent in the late 1960s, a change was inevitable.

It was not, however, at the expense of the twins. The answer was to add the 750 cc, three-cylinder Trident (see Chapter 7) to the range—and many of the features of that mighty power unit owe something to the original Speed Twin!

Chapter 7

The Trident Three

'THE DEMAND came from the USA, of course, where they wanted something that would be the biggest and best, a bike that would produce around 60 bhp and be capable of terrific acceleration.'

BSA Group chief engineer Bert Hopwood was talking soon after the 750 cc Trident had been launched. He had been primarily responsible for the design of the first Triumph with three cylinders and a capacity over 650 cc. Along with a substantially similar BSA—the Rocket 3—the Trident had appeared in September 1968. For years the 650 cc Thunderbird and Bonneville twins had been breaking sales records in the States, but the customers there were now asking for more and more power.

True, AJS, Matchless, Norton and Royal Enfield had been offering 750 cc parallel twins for some years, but the day of the superbike had arrived. The Americans wanted more performance without the vibration inseparable from the twin employing 360-degree cranks, plus refinement and luxury equipment. They were prepared to pay higher prices.

Moreover, in 1968 it was known that before very long Honda would introduce their 750 cc ohc four; the BMW R75/5 horizontally opposed twin would follow soon afterwards and the Suzuki 750 cc three-cylinder two-stroke was in the pipeline. The Trident would keep Triumph up with the competition.

There was no mistaking the Trident engine's heritage. The transverse camshafts high-placed at the front and rear of the crankcase mouth, the external push-rod tubes and the overhead-valve gear closely followed twin-cylinder practice.

Said Bert Hopwood: 'Our twin-cylinder layout was readily adaptable for three cylinders. We selected the pre-unit-construction Tiger 100 unit as the basis because it was a relatively long-stroke design and thus kept the overall width down.'

In fact, during development of the new engine, the bore and stroke were changed, with the final choice 67 mm bore against the Tiger 100's 63 mm so that bigger valves could be used.

At one stage, the three was waggishly dubbed a Tiger 100 and a half. Certainly, when they came to lay out the Trident unit Hopwood and his team called extensively on the knowledge gained in the long development of the twins.

The cylinder head was a one-piece, light-alloy casting with bolt-on, light-alloy rocker boxes and covers, one for the inlet valves, one for the exhausts. The cylinder, also, was a light-alloy block; the alloy-steel liners were pressed in and projected to form deep spigots into the crankcase. Three Amal Concentric carburettors were employed.

An unusual, yet highly successful, manufacturing method was devised for the one-piece crankshaft. The steel shaft was forged with the three cranks in one plane, then reheated and twisted to bring the cranks to the required 120-degree spacing. No flywheel was used; instead, the assembly was balanced by integral crank webs.

Of the four main bearings, the middle two were, like the big ends, of plain, shell type, with roller and ball-bearings for the timing and driving sides respectively.

To transmit the high power of the new unit, the designers were forced to abandon the usual multiplate, coil-spring clutch employed on all other models in favour of a single-plate, diaphragm-spring clutch, as in car practice. In fact, design and and production were by Borg and Beck, the car-transmission specialists, and the clutch performed admirably right from the start.

It was housed inboard of the primary drive (by triple-row chain) and in a separate, dry compartment. The primary drive had the refinement of a vane-type shock absorber and an outrigger bearing for the gearbox input shaft.

The Lucas alternator was housed in the timing chest, the rotor on the crankshaft, and the contact-breaker assembly, with three sets of points, was driven from the end of the exhaust camshaft. Unlike all the twins, which relied on double-plunger oil pumps, the Trident had a gear pump actuated by a skew drive from the exhaust camshaft, and an oil cooler was mounted just below the front of the fuel tank.

Power output was 58 bhp at 7,250 rpm, giving a top speed of over 120 mph and a time for the standing quarter-mile of just under 14 seconds.

Initially, the Trident was reserved for export only and it was received with great enthusiasm in the United States. British riders had to wait until April 1969 before deliveries started on the home market.

Soon, Tridents were being used for production-machine racing, and in the forerunners of Formula 750 events in the States with outstanding successes.

Responsible for preparing the factory racing versions was Doug Hele, who had played such an important part in the initial development programme for the machine.

Triumph first got the taste for the most famous race in the USA, the Daytona 200-miler for expert-class riders, in 1967 when Gary Nixon won riding a 500 cc twin. The Tridents were out in 1970, and Gene Romero and Don Castro brought them home in second and third places.

Romero was second again in 1971, sandwiched between Dick Mann, first, and Don Emde, third, on BSA Rocket 3s—using engines as near identical with the Trident's as no matter. That was the best year in America for the Hopwood-Hele power plant. Afterwards, with the BSA group running into deeper financial trouble, the factory racing effort was cut right back.

In Britain, Trident results were even more impressive. Malcolm Uphill won the big class of the 1970 Production Machine TT at 97.71 mph, and Tom Dickie was fourth. A year later, Ray Pickrell in winning put the average speed up to 100.07 mph; Tony Jefferies was second (a BSA Rocket 3, ridden by Bob Heath, was third), and a Boyer-modified Trident, with David Nixon up, was fifth.

That year brought the first of the Formula 750 races in the TT programme. This was another success for the Trident with Jefferies winning at 102.85 mph, and making the fastest lap at 103.21 mph. Pickrell scored the double in 1972, hoisting the lap records to 101.61 mph (Production) and 105.68 mph (Formula 750). Nixon backed up Pickrell in the Production Machine race and Jefferies did likewise with a second in the Formula 750.

Even in 1973 without factory backing, Tridents occupied the first three places in the Production race, Jefferies leading the two Boyer versions ridden by John Williams and Nixon. Tridents were also fifth and sixth. But this time the Formula 750 went to the John Player Nortons ridden by Peter Williams and Ron Grant, with Jefferies and his Trident chasing them home.

In 1974, too, the big class of the Production race fell again to a Trident, the famous Slippery Sam (see Chapter 20), this time ridden by Mick Grant. And Slippery Sam did it again in 1975 when, in a ten-lap Production TT, Dave Croxford and Alex George notched that illustrious bike's fifth win.

Apart from problems with oil leaks, dealt with by improved sealing at the crankcase and gearbox joints during the first year, the production Trident was remarkably free from troubles. It continued virtually unaltered until the introduction of the T150V in June 1972 brought the five-speed gearbox. Later that year a disc front brake, superseding the two-leading-shoe drum brake, was fitted.

Then, in January 1973, came the TRX75 Hurricane, a restyled version put into limited production primarily for the American market. This model used the BSA-type engine (cylinder block inclined slightly forward instead of vertical), a drum-type front brake, small fuel tank and revised exhaust system.

Finally, the NT160 Trident was announced in March 1975. This model, too, employed the sloping-cylinder power plant, and had disc brakes front and rear. But the T160 brought the most important technical changes so far—an electric starter and left-side gear-change pedal.

Unhappily, the production life of the T160 was destined to be all too short. 'Triumphs are rolling again,' declared the posters outside the one-time BSA works at Small Heath, but inside the factory all was far from well. Autumn brought the presentation of a petition to wind-up NVT Manufacturing Ltd, operators of the plant and, thereby, builders of the Trident (see Chapter 24).

A receiver-manager was appointed by Barclays Bank, and notices were issued to the 1,000-strong workforce. Not even an order for 200 for the Middle East could save the Trident now, and, in January 1976, the final model was assembled. It was temporarily adorned with BSA transfers, a sentimental gesture by the remaining handful of workers!

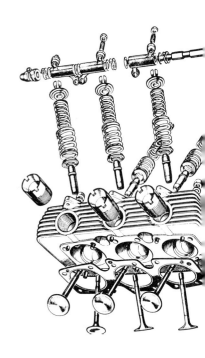

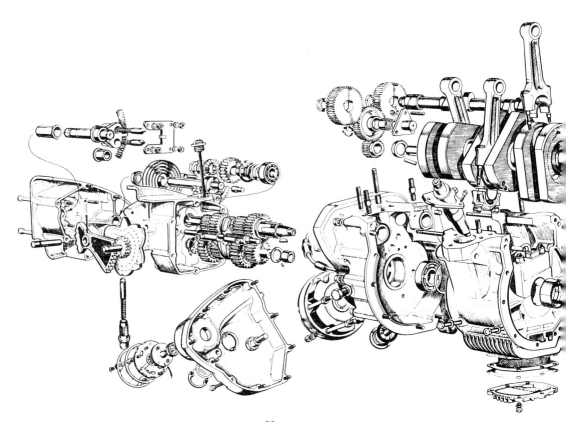

Details of the 750 cc Trident three. Light alloy is used for the cylinder head and its bolted-on rocker boxes, and for the cylinder block with pressed-in steel liners forming deep spigots into the crankcase. Crankshaft is a one-piece forging. Main bearings are roller on the timing and ball on the driving sides, plain for the middle two. Note the triple primary chain and remote, diaphragm-spring clutch, with outrigger bearing for the gearbox shaft.

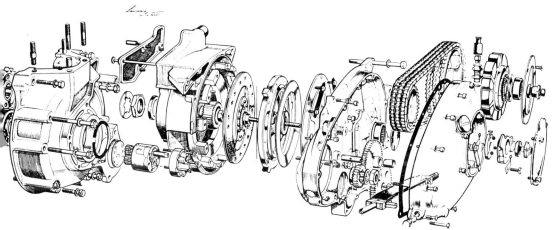

Chapter 8

On the salt

ALTHOUGH THE TRIUMPH factory rarely entered wholeheartedly into racing, from the 1950s its engines have been more popular than any other for propelling specials built by privateers to attack short-distance records.

The lead came from the United States, where sales of the Coventry-built twins were mounting steadily each year and, in California particularly, a small industry was growing up to supply modified components for giving standard Triumph engines a bit more zip.

The Americans wanted the world's glamour record—that is, the flying kilometre or mile—and, with the wide, open arena of the Bonneville Salt Flats in Utah available, they hogged the limelight from 1955.

Before then, back in the misty 1920s, the world's fastest kilometre or mile had been held by British, German and (once) Italian riders, and from 1951 the kilometre stood to the credit of Wilhelm Herz (NSU), a German, at 180 mph.

In July 1955 Russell Wright, a New Zealander, riding a home-modified 1,000 Vincent, put the speed up by 5 mph in his home country. And that was the last time any serious attempt was made anywhere but at Bonneville.

Within a few months a lanky, 26-year-old Texan, Johnny Allen, had paved the way for future attempts. He brought out a long, low, cigar-shaped streamliner with a 650 cc Triumph twin engine running on alcohol fuel, to take the American national record for the flying kilometre at 193 mph. It could not, however, be counted as a world record because the runs were not timed and supervised by officials of the international controlling body, the Fédération Internationale Motocycliste.

In July the following year, Herz and NSU returned to the fray, this time at Bonneville, and before they left in August they hoisted the record to 210 mph. This was an irresistible challenge for Allen, and on September 6 1956 he wheeled out his projectile and achieved 214.4 mph for the flying mile.

That was to prove the most controversial record claim of all time. Allen, Shorty Mangham, designer of the machine, and Jack Wilson, the engine tuner, had gone ahead on assurances that the timing and supervision of the runs were up to FIM requirements. Their claim was accepted by the FIM secretariat, subject to the usual three-month period for protests to be received. But next month, at the FIM's autumn congress in Paris, doubts were raised. The FIM asked for more information and, in April 1957, finally rejected the record claim.

For the next two years, the Triumph company in England fought a legal battle with the FIM, but failed to get satisfaction. Allen's figures never did appear in the official list.

It was an unhappy business, yet it had no real impact in the USA, where FIM jurisdiction meant little and Allen's 214.4 mph was accepted. Moreover, with the Bonneville Speed Week held each year for attempts on the long list of American-recognised records, there was every encouragement for more cracks at the world-max figures.

In September 1958 the Mangham-Triumph device was brought out again, this time handled by another Texan, 19-year-old Jess Thomas. It was fractionally faster, 214.47 mph, but no claim was put forward for world recognition. And next year, in October, Allen tried again, but crashed when travelling at over 200 mph. Apart from a few broken ribs he was, miraculously, unhurt.

The Mangham layout of a long, low, streamlined shell, the rider sitting ahead of the engine with his legs forward, was copied by others and, in late summer 1961, Joe Dudek's 17-foot-long, cigar-shaped machine appeared, piloted by Bill Johnson. It was fitted with a 600 cc Norton Dominator twin engine and, running on pump fuel, recorded over 179 mph to set a national record for its class.

By August 1962 a 650 cc Triumph Bonneville twin, alcohol-burning engine had been fitted and Johnson, now 38 years old, set the American flying-mile record at over 230 mph, the fastest of the two-way runs being at 232.26 mph.

Then, on September 5, he was out again, with timing and supervision under FIM auspices. His two-way average of 224.57 mph was an undisputed world record for Triumph, and remains unbeaten as this book goes to press.

But that is not the end of the Triumph saga in the world-fastest stakes. The FIM engine-capacity limit for recognition was then 1,000 cc. This, the Americans considered, was an irrational restriction and, anyway, they never had rated the FIM accolade very highly. They were working on double-engine specials, with rider Bob Leppan and engineer Jim Bruflodt well in the running. Their Gyronaut X-1 streamliner, styled by aerodynamicist Alex Tremulis, housed two Triumph 650 cc twin engines in tandem between the cockpit and the rear wheel. With some 120 bhp on tap and a glass-fibre shell reducing air drag to a minimum, Gyronaut was theoretically capable of up to 300 mph.

They were almost ready to go during the Bonneville Speed Week of 1964 but, as the salt surface was in poor condition, they decided against hurrying the finishing touches, intending to make a real bid a year later.

But, even then, Gyronaut was not giving its full potential. In mid-October Leppan made practice runs through the flying mile at nearly 225 mph and, on October 21, put in a two-way average of 212.65 mph to capture the American Motorcycle Association record for petrol-fuelled machines. Two days later, lubrication problems prevented an attack on Bill Johnson's figures.

The pay-off came in August 1966. With the engines fed straight alcohol, 28-year-old Bob Leppan returned a two-way average of 245.6 mph. Even so, Gyronaut would have gone faster if the run-in to the timed mile had been longer—it was accelerating all the way.

Joe Bruflodt and Bob Leppan left the salt confi-dent that next year, with the engines set up for nitro-methane fuel and a longer run-in to the timed mile, 300 mph would be possible.

That goal was not to be realised, however. Business pressure prevented Bruflodt and Leppan—they had a big Triumph agency in Detroit, Michigan—from working on Gyronaut. Then they decided to install a Trident three-cylinder engine as the intermediate stage in, finally, using two of these 750 cc power units.

The single-engine job, running on pump fuel, was out at Bonneville in August 1969 on experimental runs at just over 200 mph. But the limelight during that Speed Week was on other, less exotic, Tridents, which captured 16 American records in the various 750 cc classes recognised by the AMA.

By 1970, the two Trident engines had been installed in Gyronaut and, in October, Leppan was out to break the record of 265.5 mph which had been put up by Cal Rayborn with a Harley-Davidson-powered projectile earlier that month. But, for the first time in his high-speed career, he hit trouble. The front suspension of Gyronaut X-1 collapsed while he was travelling at 270 mph. His left arm was so seriously damaged that, at one stage, amputation seemed likely.

Leppan has recovered, but neither he nor other riders with Triumph-powered devices have since made serious attempts in the world-max stakes.

Chapter 9

Blasting off

NOT ONLY have Triumph engines figured successfully in attempts on the world's maximum-speed record, they have also been widely used for sprinting. This means standing-start runs over the quarter-mile, kilometre or mile for which, in recent years, only highly specialised machines could hope to be competitive.

In Britain, the sport enjoyed a following from the early years of motor cycling, but had to wait until the 1950s before coming into its own. In 1958, the National Sprint Association was formed and, from then on, the sport boomed. NSA membership consistently keeps over the 500 mark.

For a variety of good reasons, easily the most popular for powering the top machines in the 500 cc and larger classes is the Triumph twin. It is light yet, although not intended as a racing unit, is reliable enough when extended for no longer than the bursts of full power required in sprints. It is easy to work on and spares at reasonable prices have almost always been in good supply. In addition, high-performance equipment and components have been available from specialist firms.

At no time, though, has the Triumph factory sold engines separately for this purpose. Most sprint enthusiasts—often skilled professional or amateur engineers who build their own bikes—have had to use engines that started life in normal production roadsters, or assemble them from spares.

A glance at the data covering world and British short-distance records set during the past ten years shows a long list of names successfully linked with Triumph. Among the most prominent are Martin Roberts, Charlie Rous, Norman Hyde, Fred Cooper, Duncan Hocking, John Hobbs and three Peters—Windross, Miller and Harman.

For notching his first world record, 10.67 seconds for the standing quarter-mile at Elvington, Yorks, in October 1965, Martin Roberts employed a 650 cc Bonneville engine bored out to 663 cc and supercharged by a blower chain-driven from the crankshaft. Large-diameter top, front and seat tubes were a feature of the robust but simple, unsprung frame, and sturdy, perforated plates were fitted to stiffen the engine and gearbox mountings. The top tube of the frame served as a fuel tank.

Roberts' machine is just one example of a straightforward, Triumph-engined sprinter achieving terrific acceleration from a high power-to-weight ratio and expert use of the power characteristics by the rider.

But sprint specials come in much more complicated and massive form, as Fred Cooper showed with his 1,267 cc Cyclotron, first seen on the strips in October 1967. As did Bob Leppan in Gyronaut X-1 (see Chapter 8), which had achieved nearly 246 mph for the American flying-mile record a year earlier, Cooper employed two Triumph 650 cc twin engines in tandem. They were geared together and supercharged by a Shorrock blower driven from the front crankshaft through a cogged belt.

The odd capacity of the engine, 1,267 cc, illustrates the versatility of sprint men in building hybrids. Cooper married a pair of six-fifty cylinder blocks (71 mm bore) with crankshaft assemblies from 500 cc engines (80 mm stroke) to leave a margin for cylinder wear without exceeding the FIM 1,300 cc capacity limit, as could easily happen, with the 82 mm stroke of the six-fifty crank giving a capacity nearer 1,299 than 1,298 cc.

The shorter stroke served another purpose. With supercharging, a slightly lower compression ratio than the standard 9 to 1 was required. The pistons ran 1 mm lower at top dead centre and gave 8 to 1!

Unlike the others before him who had used two engines, Cooper decided on gears for coupling the crankshafts instead of a chain. In conjunction with special crankshafts having throws at 180 degrees instead of the standard 360 degrees, the firing order was rear piston right, rear left, front right, and front left. This kept the snatch frequency on the coupling gears to a minimum. However, later in the development of Cyclotron, the gears proved unreliable, and chain coupling was adopted.

Cooper's fame was built on his sprinting exploits riding Hermes, a 500 cc single-engined machine with which he gained world records for the standing-start quarter-mile and mile in the mid-1960s. Cyclotron, though suitable for sprinting, was envisaged also as being basically right for an attack on Bob Leppan's American max record.

At one stage the *Daily Express* promised to sponsor Cooper on a trip to the Bonneville Salt Flats in the United States for the attack, provided he could first achieve a certified 200 mph on a British strip. Cooper never made it and eventually retired from the fray, but not before he had set, among other records, 187.34 mph for the flying kilometre (in September 1972) and 189.87 mph for the flying quarter-mile (a year later), in the 1,300 cc class.

Yet another application of Triumph engines—in this case, two 500 cc twins—was seen in John Hobbs' Olympus II that started snatching records in 1972. The big talking point was that Hobbs employed not only two engines but two blowers as well; all other examples had utilised one blower to serve the four cylinders.

The reason was simple. On his earlier machine, Olympus I, he had had eight years of experience in developing the 500 cc supercharged Triumph engine. Olympus I, at that time, held three world and four British records, and was the only five-hundred to have got below 10 seconds for the standing quarter-mile. The engines which had been used in Olympus I were installed in the big bike, though the cylinder head of the front one was reversed (inlet ports to the front, exhausts to the rear) and its supercharger was housed in front of the crankcase instead of behind the cylinder block. Both the Shorrock blowers were driven by double vee-belts, and the crankshafts were coupled by a chain.

Although Hobbs foresaw a lot of trial-and-error development throughout the summer of 1972, by the September records meeting at Elvington his new creation was going well enough to take the world standing-start quarter-mile, kilometre and mile records. But like so many sprint enthusiasts who enjoy the mechanical work of modifying and developing almost as much as burning up the strips, Hobbs decided in mid-1973 to up the capacity to 1,500 cc by using Morgo engine conversions. At Elvington in September the bigger Olympus II recorded 10.62 seconds for the standing quarter, and made 9.64 seconds, one way, at the final—and wet—Santa Pod meeting of the year. And at Elvington, incidentally, no one bettered the records that had been set by the 1,000 cc version a year earlier.

Olympus II was in even better form in 1974. In June one-way runs at Santa Pod, Hobbs made a best for the standing quarter-mile in 9.17 seconds then, in July, 9.16 seconds, with a terminal speed of 155.28 mph.

But perhaps the most astonishing Triumph-powered sprint achievement came in June 1975 when Keith Parnell, using only one 750 cc twin-cylinder engine in his special machine, recorded 8.93 seconds one way at Santa Pod and became the first European rider to better nine seconds for the standing quarter-mile.

Chapter 10

Blown before

WHETHER FOR record-attempting, sprinting or grass-track sidecar racing, the supercharged Triumph-twin power unit is now so common that it excites little more than passing interest. But back in the 1930s a blown Triumph was rare indeed—and a factory-prepared specimen even rarer.

In the two decades between the wars it seemed almost as though *The Motor Cycle* had become obsessed with the 100-miles-in-the-hour theme. The magazine's first venture was to offer a magnificent trophy to be won by the first rider to cover 100 miles in an hour with a British machine on British soil. That was no easy task because the only suitable venue was Brooklands. This concrete bowl was very bumpy, and an even bigger handicap was that the machines had to be fitted with regulation silencers.

However, the trophy was won in August 1928 by Bill Laccy on his immaculate, 500 cc single-cylinder Grindlay Peerless JAP, with an average speed of 103.3 mph.

So *The Motor Cycle* offered another trophy, this time for the first ton-hour performance on a multi-cylinder five-hundred. Several companies and individual riders decided to have a go, among them Triumph, whose Val Page-designed 650 cc vertical twin had just been launched. The silverware was for up-to-500 cc machines only, but there was no reason why one of the Page engines should not be cut down to size. The work was entrusted to Ernie Nott and the competition-experimental department, and what emerged was far more than a mere exercise in cylinder sleeving.

To reduce the capacity, they settled for 63 × 80 mm because these were the dimensions of the then-current 250 cc single, and it permitted Nott to use the two-fifty's pistons, valves and other components. It meant, too, that a standard 650 cc cylinder-block casting, underbored but not linered, could be fitted.

To withstand the extra loads from supercharging with alcohol fuel, the crankshaft was not only given shorter throws; diameters were increased all round and the shaft was carried in a roller bearing each side. The drive-side shaft was lengthened, and projected into an outrigger ball-bearing mounted in the special primary-drive case.

Because the Zoller supercharger was mounted behind the cylinder block, the magneto was transferred to the front of the engine and a suitable drive arranged. The engine employed double-helical primary gearing, and the drive for the supercharger was meshed with the clutch gear. The supercharger gear was supported by a double-row roller bearing carried in the drive-case casting, and connected to the blower shaft through a splined coupling (in fact, part of a Triumph quickly detachable rear-wheel hub suitably adapted).

The Zoller was intended for a 1,100 cc engine and, therefore, it was geared to run at two-thirds engine speed. Delivery pressure was between 7 and 10 psi and the pistons gave a 7.5-to-1 compression ratio. Carburation was by a 1⅛ inch-choke Amal, and on the test bench the engine produced 46.7 bhp at 4,600 rpm. The top gear ratio of 3.78 to 1 would give 100 mph at 4,700 rpm.

To improve both the pressure and the quantity of oil circulated, a larger-than-standard pump was employed; a separate, small oil pump with tank was provided for supercharger lubrication. The gearbox was equipped with a stiffened mainshaft running in roller bearings, and an additional friction plate—making five—was added to the clutch.

Except that the seat tube had to be offset slightly to clear the intake, the frame was that of the standard six-fifty twin, but the link-type front fork came from the 5/10 model, the over-the-counter racer of the Triumph range. Over all sat a six-gallon fuel tank, in glittering copper plating. The effect was both neat and striking.

The mass onslaught to win the trophy began one Tuesday in May 1934, with ACU timekeeper George Reynolds in charge of the watches. Former TT winner Charlie Dodson (on the works vee-twin New Imperial), Ben Bickell (supercharged Ariel Square Four) and Tom Atkins (Douglas twin) were ready to take a turn.

Nearest to success was Dodson, who had begun to lap consistently at over 103 mph when, on the 13th round and with half a minute in hand on his schedule, the front exhaust-pipe flange broke off. It was very evident to the Triumph crew that, unless they did something very quickly, the New Imperial camp would collar the trophy.

And so, with Harry Perrey in charge and Tommy Spann as rider, the special Triumph was at Brooklands on Friday of the same week. Though the engine had performed well enough on the test bench, the built-up bike had not been run, and trouble came at a very early stage.

Spann had gone out for a few practice laps at 100 mph but, all too soon, was back in the pits calling for a change of sparking plugs. Out he went again, but had to return a second time for the same reason. Then it was noticed that centrifugal fling was causing the rear-tyre tread to make contact with a projecting mudguard bolt. The bolt was changed, a new tyre fitted, and even colder plugs were screwed home. Spann tried again and, ripping off a couple of laps at over 100 mph with the ignition bothers seemingly cured, was ready to go for the trophy.

From a standing start he put in a 92.57-mph lap, and then upped it to 104 mph next time round. Ten laps were completed, but on the last two the average speed dropped to little over 100 mph. In came the Triumph, running on only one cylinder, and that was that.

'On our own, with no timekeepers about,' reminisced Harry Perrey years later, 'the blown twin lapped at 116 mph. We knew it had all the potential necessary to win the trophy. But the magneto just wasn't man enough for the job. The pressures in the combustion chambers just blew out the sparks, so to speak. First the engine would start to run on one cylinder only, then it would fluff out altogether. The magneto people blamed the failure on us—said we hadn't given them enough information on our requirements.'

However, not all the troubles could be blamed on ignition. The short intake coupling between the supercharger and the cylinder head resulted in uneven distribution of gas between the two cylinders; there was a complete absence of any cushioning effect. Should the throttle be opened suddenly, the engine would choke.

A few improvements were made, and the crew returned to Brooklands for another attempt, on Wednesday, August 1. Steady laps at 105 mph were achieved—but it was already too late. Also at the track that day were the full New Imperial race-shop crew headed by Matt Wright and Les Archer senior, and the company's managing director, Norman Downs. In the saddle, this time, was carburettor wizard Stan (Ginger) Wood. With a faultless run on the New Imperial 492 cc vee-twin, he claimed *The Motor Cycle* trophy at 102.21 mph. It was the 37th time a twin had made an attempt to achieve the 100-mph hour and, said George Reynolds, his watches had recorded some 257 laps, successful or otherwise—the total did not, of course, take into account the untimed practice runs.

The target at which all the effort had been aimed had now disappeared, but the works blown Triumph had one more part to play. Converted to roadgoing trim, it reappeared in 1935 as a test bed for supercharging experiments then being carried out by M. A. McEvoy Ltd, of Derby. It blossomed with a long induction pipe which passed right round the front of the engine. Blower pressure had been raised to 15 psi, and compression ratio lowered to 5.5 to 1. The McEvoy experiments were concerned with the development of supercharging for roadster machines and, accordingly, the fuel used was petrol, not alcohol.

'The acceleration,' said a member of the staff of *Motor Cycling* after riding the McEvoy version, 'has to be experienced to be believed. It is no exaggeration to say that when the throttle is opened suddenly it takes a considerable effort on the rider's part to remain on the machine and not be left behind.'

However, nothing further was made known, and the special twin disappeared into oblivion. Nevertheless, another supercharged twin made an appearance at Brooklands before the famous circuit was closed on the coming of war. It was a 500 cc Speed Twin and, through the winter of 1937-38, owner Maurice Winslow and road-racer Ivan Wicksteed had worked steadily to convert it to supercharged form. Again the blower was mounted above the gearbox, but the drive was by chain.

For the annual Hutchinson 100 meeting at Brooklands the British Motor Cycle Racing Club had arranged a very varied programme, including quarter-mile sprints and attempts at 100-mph laps. But it was a cold and rain-lashed day in October, hardly conducive to successful record breaking.

Undaunted by the wet and howling south-west gale, Ivan Wicksteed was pushed away for his attack on the Brooklands Class C (500 cc), flying-lap record. The sound of his engine echoed back from the concrete slopes as he battled his way round on the run-in—then he was across the line and into his officially timed lap.

He registered 1 minute 24.4 seconds. That was the equivalent of 118.02 mph, and Denis Minett's record had been smashed by nearly $1\frac{3}{4}$ mph.

In just under a year Brooklands was to close for ever, so Wicksteed's 500 cc record on the blown Speed Twin stands in perpetuity—together with the 750 cc and 350 cc class records, also held by Triumph machines.

Chapter 11

The American connection

ADDICTS OF HOLLYWOOD gangster movies (and, for that matter, of Laurel and Hardy comedies) will confirm that, in the 1930s, the native American motor cycle was very much alive and kicking. It was a massive vee-twin, of either Harley-Davidson or Indian origin, and it could be found lurking behind a billboard on the outskirts of any one-horse township you care to name. The rider, of course, was a typically impassive, gum-chewing cop.

A true picture? No, not quite. Though their numbers were relatively small, 'cycle nuts' were still around and, indeed, there were even a few small-production makes such as the Crocker. Perhaps it was only natural that the largest pool of two-wheel enthusiasm should be found on the sunny West Coast, and it is appropriate that this part of the Triumph story should start on a street in Pasadena, California.

There, one day in 1939, a local motor cyclist named Bill Johnson spotted an unfamiliar machine parked by the kerb and, on stopping to examine it, discovered it to be a British-made Ariel Square Four. Bill was so enchanted that he imported a Square Four for himself—then, later, a few more to sell to fellow enthusiasts in the Los Angeles area. From this transaction there ripened an acquaintanceship by correspondence between Johnson, in California, and Edward Turner, designer of the Square Four, in England, that continued throughout the war years.

With the lifting of restrictions, the two formed a close personal and business relationship. Edward found Bill's easy-going and relaxed Western humour attractive, and Bill, with his deep perception, sensed Edward's genius in technical matters. Turner had long been an admirer of America and, soon, he came to regard the West Coast as his second home.

Specialising in Ariel and Triumph machines, Bill Johnson went into business as a dealer, with a handsome showroom and service centre on the main street of Pasadena. By the end of 1946, some 500 Triumph machines had been imported into the the USA, and all but a handful of them were sold through Johnson Motors Inc.

But it was becoming evident that though California, with its pleasant climate, was an excellent nursery area for an open-air sport such as motor cycling, there was a much greater sales potential in the heavily populated middle America, the southern states, and in the Atlantic seaboard regions.

To sound out the potential, Edward Turner brought into consultation another motor-cycle enthusiast and old friend, Percival White, president of the Market Research Corporation of America. A collector of technically interesting motor cycles, and a great Douglas fanatic, Percival White had virtually pioneered the science of market research, had written text books on the subject, and was in demand as a university lecturer.

On the staff of the Market Research Corporation, in charge of European accounts, was one Denis McCormack. Here, too, was a man whose roots lay in the motor-cycle world for McCormack, born in Coventry in 1901, had joined the Beardmore Precision factory at King's Norton, Birmingham, on leaving school. From there he went to Wolseley Motors, and then across the Atlantic to a number of jobs—which included a brief interlude as a consultant, trying to unravel the dying Indian company's post-war, and never-to-be-realised, plans.

The Market Research Corporation's studies confirmed Turner's hopes. Yes, prospects for a substantial market for the distinctive 'English-style' motor cycle were encouraging, and Triumph had the right machine for the market. The recommendations were that West Coast marketing should be left in the capable hands of Johnson Motors Inc (who were now importing Triumphs at the rate of 1,000 a year), but that a new organisation to take care of the rest of the country should be set up. This should be based in the East, and be under the control of the parent Triumph Engineering Company, of Meriden.

Together with Triumph chairman Jack Sangster, Turner travelled to the USA in 1950 for final consultation with Denis McCormack who, Percival White agreed, should be released from the Market Research Corporation to become president, general manager and sales manager of the proposed new Triumph Corporation of America.

A preliminary six-month period was spent in laying out detail plans, assembling a working team, finding suitable premises, and completing legal and banking arrangements. On the Atlantic seaboard, halfway between the north and south,

Baltimore, Maryland, was chosen as the home of the new corporation, because of the efficiency of its port installations, and its superior road and rail connections to the mid-western states.

The immediate and logical choice as service manager was Rod Coates, who had just won the Daytona 100-mile Amateur Championship on a 500 cc Triumph Grand Prix. Rod had a sound practical engineering background, and was to prove well worth the ransom necessary to pry him loose from the then-independent BSA importer, Alf Childs.

Other recruits to the team included Jack Mercer as chief field representative, Phyllis Fansler, who was to run the orders department with great efficiency, and Earl Miller as accountant and McCormack's right-hand man.

Co-director and a long-time associate of Denis McCormack, lawyer John Wright provided the sound legal guidance that kept the Triumph Corporation, in its extremely active first 17 years of growth, out of lawsuits of any nature, and helped also in establishing the corporation's firm standing with the banks and financial institutions.

Trading began in 1951 on a modest scale, with but a handful of dealers transferred from the fringes of the Johnson Motors franchise. The budget was necessarily low, but by concentrating on the job in hand a small profit was made, even in that opening year. Indeed, total imports of Triumph models to the USA (including those for Johnson Motors) had more than doubled and, at 2,730 machines, were valued at over £680,000.

However, the first years were by no means easy. Business systems and facilities had to be evolved. The motor cycles themselves had to be modified repeatedly, to keep the specifications in line with the American rider's requirements. In this respect, Edward Turner's deep understanding of America, and the patient co-operation at Meriden of men such as Bert Hopwood, Jack Wicks, John Nelson and Bill Robertson, were important factors.

Some discouragement came from the attitude of the native motor-cycle industry which, by this time, was represented almost exclusively by Milwaukee's Harley-Davidson Motor Company. The old Indian company, originally larger than Harley-Davidson, had declined and was no longer important.

With the return of peace, Harley-Davidson had settled back in 1946 to resume its dominance of American motor cycling—but was shocked to discover a challenger and, in particular, one from overseas. To them, the appearance of the vastly

experienced Triumph Engineering Co, with its factory-owned branch at Baltimore, was a threat to their market.

They complained forcefully in the American press and in their own advertising. They attempted to stop Harley-Davidson dealers from having anything to do with Triumph or any of the other imported makes then appearing on the American scene, and threatened to withdraw recognition from any dealer who showed any inclination towards taking up a Triumph agency. They tried to bar Triumph field representatives from even entering the premises of accredited Harley dealers.

In this way, the older-established dealers in the USA were cut off from contact with the new mediumweight, high-performance type of motor cycle, and the only outlets Triumph could find were dealers fired by Harley-Davidson (or who had left the Harley network in protest), and the remnants of the now bankrupt Indian organisation.

Triumph at Baltimore and Johnson in California began training and service schools for new dealers— principally young ex-servicemen seeking to start in business with a few thousand dollars of gratuity money or with loans from friends or family sources.

The schools gave tuition in the unfamiliar mechanics and electrics of British models and taught, also, business procedures such as finance, book-keeping and good customer relations. There was, too, guidance in the tuning of Triumph engines for competition work and in the promotion of sporting events.

Several hundred new dealers, staff employees and sales representatives passed through the schools and became the nucleus of the great expansion and successful growth of the Triumph organisation in the USA. Throughout, there was encouragement from Edward Turner, with many personal visits (during which he was in great demand as an after-dinner speaker).

The impact of Triumph—and, to a lesser degree, of BSA—led Harley-Davidson to place a formal plea for protection before the Tariff Commission in Washington in 1952. For the previous 20 years the import duty on foreign-made motor cycles had stood at 10 per cent, but H-D now asked for it to be raised to 40 per cent and, in addition, for a quota system whereby the number of machines should be a given percentage of the number that they (H-D) could make and sell.

With the assistance of Jack Sangster, who provided ammunition in the form of comparative labour and material costs, Denis McCormack organised Triumph's defence before the Tariff

Commissioner. The legal costs of preparing a brief were daunting, but there was financial assistance from other importing concerns, and notable support was given by the editor of the now-defunct motor-cycle magazine, *Buzzz*.

Except for a 125 cc lightweight (derived from the same pre-war DKW design as the BSA Bantam), Harley-Davidson's only offerings to the American motor cyclist at this time were the expensive vee-twins of 1,000 cc and larger, weighing over 750 lb. It was astonishing that the Milwaukee factory should have hoped to continue to dominate the market with these two extreme and semi-obsolete machines—especially when thousands of prospective riders were returning from service in Europe, where they had seen the products of British factories.

Triumph's plea to the Tariff Commission was that their products—moderate in price, light in weight and of high efficiency—stood midway between Harley's big twins and lightweights. The Triumphs, therefore, filled a market sector which Harley-Davidson had either chosen to ignore, or didn't know existed, and could not be considered the 'unfair trade practice' that H-D had charged.

After a couple of weeks of hearings in Washington, the Tariff Commission instructed Harley-Davidson to compete by normal commercial methods—but there was still the matter of the H-D company's attitude concerning its dealers. So, a year or two later, it was the Milwaukee firm's turn to stand on the mat and face an 'unfair-trading' charge.

Again the hearings were lengthy, but the outcome was that Harley-Davidson was ordered to stop inserting 'exclusivity' clauses in dealer contracts, and to refrain from taking punitive measures against H-D dealers who wanted to stock competitors' products.

Thus was won freedom for the importer and dealer. Later, when Japan began to export to the USA, the concessionaires were able to take advantage of a well-established and experienced countrywide dealer industry.

In one further arena, Triumph had to fight for recognition. The American Motorcycle Association, with its allied Motorcycle Trade Association, also seemed to take an unfavourable view of the Triumph concern. Consequently, the Triumph Corporation's formal requests to be allowed to take a proper share of the deliberations and responsibilities were regularly rejected. But it could only be a matter of time before the growing strength of, and rider preference for, the imported product forced a capitulation and, under the enlightened secretaryship of Lynn Kuchler, both

Triumph and BSA became members of the Motor Cycle Trade Association.

By the end of 1954, the value of machines shipped from Meriden had risen to over £1,000,000, and the Triumph Corporation had outgrown its leased premises in Joppa Road, Baltimore. Accordingly, a fine new sales, service and warehouse building was erected on a prominent ten-acre site in the Towson area of Baltimore, just off the new Baltimore Beltway ring road.

It was a proud day for Triumph when, in 1955, Edward Turner declared the new premises open, in the presence of a distinguished gathering of governmental officials, and representatives from the industry and the banking and legal professions. All the prejudices and growing pains had been overcome and the green light was showing brightly. Through the next, and the third five-year periods, progress and profit in the American market were to be more rewarding, and the dedication of the employees was to create an excellent importer-dealer relationship. That happy family is still lovingly recalled by those who struggle with the problems of today's sterner conditions.

By 1963, Triumph exports to the USA were running at 6,300 machines. Four years later, that had leaped to 24,600 motor cycles with a total value of around £7,500,000.

Though there was considerable opposition from Edward Turner, the American branches of Triumph (and, to a lesser extent, BSA) took the racing and competition route as a substantial proportion of their publicity budget. In the East and West, respectively, the racing side was handled by Rod Coates and Pete Coleman, and they in turn were spurred on by the strong rivalry between Eastern and Western riders which has marked the American racing scene for many years.

In the beginning, the mainstay of Triumph's invasion of America was the 650 cc Thunderbird of 1950, followed up by the new, light-alloy 500 cc Tiger sports models. The merits of these machines were well exploited by the sales-promotion and marketing methods developed by the Triumph organisation. Also, the marketing was backed by a very superior parts supply and technical service for dealers. Triumph in America became a legend, and the strength and loyalty of its dealers proved invaluable when, in later years, the competition became more severe, the guidance and engineering genius of Edward Turner was no longer available, and management on both sides of the Atlantic had passed into other hands.

The impact of the Japanese onslaught began to be felt in the mid-1960s, at which time Japan was concentrating on smaller-capacity models from 50 to 250 cc, initially by Honda, Yamaha and Suzuki. Extensive and brilliant advertising convinced a whole new market that motor cycling was socially acceptable, and it was a compliment to the systems and policies of the Triumph Corporation that the personnel employed by the Japanese manufacturers on their entry into the American market were, in many instances, graduates of the Triumph organisation there.

The Triumph range had never been strong in lightweights (the 200 cc Tiger Cub, unhappily, was dropped in 1968) and had there been a first-class 350 cc Turner-designed machine to supplement the larger-capacity models the ultimate story might have been different. A machine of this type was urged by the Triumph Corporation of America, but the home factory's reply was that it was no longer possible to produce machines of 350 cc or under in Britain to compete with the hordes of low-price lightweights now pouring in from Japan.

However, the new market exploited by the Japanese factories did have a beneficial effect on sales of Triumph's own specialities in the 650 cc class. Having sampled the lightweights, the new motor cyclists looked around for something more powerful, and Triumph filled that need—for a while.

But, from 1965 onward, Japanese manufacturers were expanding successfully into the larger-engine section of the market. The severity of the competition, the failure of the BSA Group to introduce acceptable new designs, and the withdrawal from top management of the former team began to show.

As seen from America by Denis McCormack, the top management fomented unnecessary rivalry between Triumph at Meriden and BSA at Small Heath. But there was, also, much criticism and a growing lack of confidence among dealers in the USA, who saw only too well that Triumph—and, even more so, BSA—had lost the magic touch.

Incomprehensible to those in America, says Denis McCormack, was the setting-up of the research and development centre at Umberslade Hall. It housed a varied assembly of around 250 engineers, many without any practical experience of motor-cycle design. Unfortunately, they failed to make use of such motor-cycle men of long experience who still remained within the group.

The grandiose Umberslade programme was allowed to run its course, while the Americans begged for the release of something—anything—saleable. The call was answered, but more from the engineering staff left at the factories than from Umberslade, with the excellent Triumph-BSA three-cylinder machines designed and put into production by chief engineer Bert Hopwood, a man with long experience of design under Turner.

Reshuffles of key personnel in the early 1970s failed to produce the superman who, by this time, was needed if the motor-cycle division of the BSA group was to return to prosperity. No longer able to carry the cost of a separate brand-name market promotion, BSA, the weaker of the two makes, expired in 1972.

In the spring of 1973, the bankruptcy which was about to overtake the group was averted at the 11th hour by a merger with Norton in a new company, Norton Villiers Triumph Limited.

The new company planned to replace the past loss-making motor-cycle operation by a profitable concentration of production of Triumph and Norton in two factories only, Birmingham and Wolverhampton, involving the closure of Meriden at the end of 1973. The workforce there refused to accept the plan and blockaded the factory.

After September 1973, no Triumphs were produced for seven months until the Birmingham factory could be retooled to manufacture the complete Trident instead of only the engine which had been made there for some years.

The merger called for amalgamation of the Triumph and Norton distribution organisation in the USA. Considerable economies were necessary on the Triumph side, following the dearth of machines resulting from the blockade. The headquarters and all administration were concentrated in Duarte, California, in the modern building opened by Lord Snowdon in 1965. The Norton headquarters at Long Beach, California, and the old BSA Inc headquarters at Verona, New Jersey, were closed, while the Baltimore building continued for the time being as a warehouse and parts distribution centre for the East. At the same time, the corporate structure was streamlined into two companies only, Norton Triumph Corporation and Top Gear Inc, a subsidiary firm to promote clothing, accessories and goodies.

When Meriden Motor Cycles acquired NVT's overseas franchises in mid-1977, the arrangement included the Californian organisation of NVT which, meanwhile, had moved to Anaheim. MMC soon switched the Triumph operation to Placentia, some six miles away.

Chapter 12

Settling down

THOUGH THE FAMOUS 'Trusty' slogan (which came to be used, also, as the firm's telegraphic address) originated among the dispatch riders of the First World War, it might well have been applied right from the start. In overall control of the technical side, Mauritz Schulte was conservative in his engineering outlook and, in consequence, for at least a couple of decades the Triumph reputation rested more on sound workmanship and solid dependability than on technical innovation.

Certainly, the factory's entry into the powered world in 1902 was a remarkably cautious one. Two years earlier the Belgian Minerva company had patented a compact little engine which, when carried ahead of the front down tube of a normal bicycle, gave a limited degree of motorisation.

Minerva began to ship the little $1\frac{3}{4}$ hp (66 × 70 mm) units to Britain, tempting several bicycle manufacturers to try them out, and Triumph followed convention by clipping the engine to a standard frame, with direct drive to a belt rim attached to the spokes of the rear wheel.

As was common at that time, the engine had an automatic inlet valve and, for present-day riders, this may need explanation. The exhaust valve was operated in the usual way by a cam running at half crankshaft speed, but the inlet valve was merely held on to its seating by a light coil spring. As the piston descended on the induction stroke, the valve was sucked open against spring pressure, to admit a fresh charge of gas.

Not only that, but the machine was equipped with what was euphemistically termed a surface carburettor. This was a small tank in which petrol was swilled around by the motion of the bike. Vapour arising from the agitated petrol was collected by a current of air passing across the surface, and drawn into the combustion chamber.

It was all very hit-and-miss, and the conventional bicycle pedalling gear was there for the very real purpose of providing assistance to the engine on anything other than a dead-level highway. Pioneer riders just had to be athletic.

There was again a Minerva engine for 1903 and, although the frame remained as before, unstrutted in any way, the power unit had progressed to cam operation of both valves, while the crude surface carburettor had been replaced by a French-built Longuemare spray carburettor. Like its predecessor, the second Triumph was equipped with a contracting-band brake on the rear hub, and this feature was continued for several years to come.

Now came the first true Triumph motor cycle, as opposed to a converted bicycle; the factory launched into a three-model range for 1904, each with the engine carried upright in a diamond frame. There were $2\frac{1}{2}$ and 3 hp solos, plus a forecar powered by a water-cooled 3 hp engine. Minerva had been thrown over, and the new power units had automatic inlet valves. Belgium was still the country of origin of the 3 hp engines, but they were made by Fafnir (with, interestingly enough, a reported output of 3 bhp at 1,800 rpm).

The $2\frac{1}{2}$ hp model represented the first Triumph of entirely British construction, for its engine was a JAP, produced in the London factory of J. A. Prestwich. However, it did not make a hit with the general public; in a press advertisement for March 1905, surplus stocks of the JAP model were being offered at a clearance price of £30.

By that time Schulte had discarded the proprietary-engine policy and had settled for a one-model programme, the special significance of which was that the bike was for the first time completely of Triumph design and manufacture. It was the legendary 'three-horse', probably the first truly reliable motor cycle to be put on sale, and its introduction could hardly have come at a more propitious time.

With very few exceptions, early motor cycles had been high-built and unwieldy, as well as being unreliable mechanically. Triumph changed all that, and in doing so breathed new life into the motor cycle movement, which had been heading for premature extinction.

Overall responsibility for the machine lay with Schulte, but it appears likely that the true designer was Charles Hathaway. Capacity was 298 cc (78 × 76 mm), and there were cam operated side valves and a Brown and Barlow carburettor. The crankshaft was mounted in ball-bearings—the first recorded use of such an arrangement.

The weakest part of the machine was the frame (Registered Design No 429114) for, although the tandem front down tubes looked robust, they were to be proved otherwise when put to the test. Though now strutted, the front fork remained completely devoid of springing.

'Lightest on the market,' claimed Triumph advertisements for their 3 hp model. At only 125 lb, that could well have been so. As fitted to the earlier models, Waterson accumulator-and-coil ignition was specified for the cheaper (£43) model, but magneto ignition was available, for the first time, on the dearer (£50) version. Still-existing records indicate that production reached five machines a week.

Patented in the joint names of Hathaway and the Triumph company, the horizontal-spring front fork had been undergoing tests in the early part of 1905; results were satisfactory, and it was introduced into the range for 1906, together with a heftier single-tube frame evolved after the troubles encountered with the tandem-tube type. Minor improvements were made to the piston and valves but, excellent though the 3 hp model now was, there were better things to come.

In the autumn of 1906, spectators at the Auto Cycle Club's hill-climb at Dashwood, in the Chilterns, were startled when Triumph works rider Frank Hulbert appeared from the pits with something new—and proceeded to carve 7 seconds off the hill-climb record on his first ride.

The newcomer was the development prototype of a 3½ hp model that was to replace the 3 hp for 1907. Except that the top tube of the frame was raked rearward to lower the saddle height, it looked pretty much like its predecessor, but internally the engine had the unusual feature of stamped, steel flywheel discs with cast-iron rims. In the course of the year, over 1,000 of the 3½ hp models were to be dispatched from the Priory Street plant. Yet already a successor was in course of preparation.

Again, the public had seen it quite early in the development stage, though they may not have realised it. In fact, the 1908 3½ hp motor cycle was based on the machine which Coventry publican Jack Marshall rode into second place in the 1907 TT, the first meeting of that famous series. To take better advantage of the TT regulations, the bore of Marshall's engine had been enlarged from 82 to 84 mm, so pushing up the capacity from 450 to 475 cc, and those dimensions were to stay unchanged for the next couple of years.

Typical of Schulte's thoroughness, the production models had cylinders cast from brass patterns, to achieve uniformity of cylinder-wall thickness. New, too, was a tandem-barrel carburettor of Triumph's own design, and speed was now controlled by cable from a handlebar lever, instead of by rod from a kind of chess-bishop clipped to the frame top tube. Marshall had dispensed with pedal

gear on his TT racer, but it was retained on the production models.

If the customer wished, a Sturmey-Archer three-speed hub (in essence, a robust version of the type still manufactured for bicycle use) could be fitted at extra cost, but the more normal offering was a variable pulley giving a ratio choice of either 4 to 1 or 6 to 1. (The change of ratio could not be made with the machine on the move. The rider had to dismount, unship the toolkit and dismantle the pulley, select the ratio he required and shorten or lengthen the belt to suit, then reassemble everything and restart.)

Production was now galloping ahead, and no fewer than 3,000 Triumphs were made in 1909. In the previous July, a works-development model equipped with a metal-to-metal multi-plate clutch made its début in the ACU Six Days Trial, and later became available as production was stepped up.

The clutch was located inside the rear hub, and a Triumph stationary, but with the engine running and (apparently) the rear belt rim revolving independently of the wheel, presented a rather odd sight. At around the same time, the factory saw fit to patent a brass syringe which, carried in a holder on the saddle tube, was intended for drawing oil from the tank and squirting it to various bearings; riders soon found that, if filled with petrol instead, it was of more benefit in freeing the multiplicity of plates in the hub clutch. Triumph clutch stiction problems go back a very, very long way!

Again the TT races were used as a testing ground, and the 1909 event saw the appearance of a 3½ hp machine with still bigger dimensions. The 84 × 86 mm bore and stroke gave 499 cc, and the model was the harbinger of the next season's range.

Two types of machine were shown in the Triumph catalogue. For the sportier lads, there was a TT job, without pedalling gear and having a remarkably short (49½ inch) wheelbase. It could be had in stripped racer or road-equipped form. Pedal gear was still featured on the longer-wheelbase touring model, available with or without the Triumph hub clutch.

With the departure of the production line, the Much Park Street works had turned in part to sidecar manufacture, and now Rowland Tomson evolved and patented a chassis and body design that was generations ahead of its time. The body was torpedo-shaped, and suspended on springs within an enveloping chassis loop—very much like the Steib and Blacknell layouts of modern times.

In motor-cycle development, however, Triumph in the final years before the outbreak of the 1914-18 war had slowed to a walk. The machines were still craftsman-built, good-looking and utterly reliable, but they were being left astern in technical innovation by their competitors.

However, Schulte and his design team had not been idle, and even though an ingenious epicyclic countershaft gearbox, and a very advanced side-valve vertical twin, failed to get beyond the prototype stage, a new and very different Triumph was put before the public in November 1913.

Surprisingly, it was a two-stroke, a simple 225 cc (64 × 70 mm) machine with a two-speed gearbox operated by cable from a handlebar lever, but innocent of any such refinement as a clutch. The rider just sat astride it, snicked into gear, and paddled off. Engine, gearbox and magneto formed a handy subunit that could be lifted out of the frame and on to the workbench when repairs were called for.

Slung below the frame top tube by two nickel-plated straps, the cylindrical fuel tank incorporated a compartment for lubricating oil; beneath was a tap whereby the oil could be drawn off as required into a measure integral with the filler cap, and then tipped into the fuel compartment to make the petroil. Perhaps it should be added that, when production began in April 1914, the oil tap (which, it was found, could vibrate open) had been replaced by a hand-pump device.

Both designer Charles Hathaway and tester Frank Hulbert enthused about the little Junior, which the public at large soon nicknamed the Baby (because, said the funny men, it never went out without its rattle). Further testimony came from Schulte's younger daughter, Muriel, who claimed the prototype for her own use. Solemnly, Muriel Schulte was entered in the Triumph sales ledger as the first Junior customer.

For 1914 the stroke of the big four-stroke had been lengthened to 97 mm on the roadster models, bringing the capacity to 550 cc (the TT model remained at 499 cc), and this size of engine was to be featured in the Triumph programme for many years ahead. But soon Europe was to be plunged into conflict, and there were more important items to occupy the newspaper headlines than a new bike from Triumph.

All the same, the machine that went into production in the closing weeks of 1914 was a landmark in the company's history. Though based on the 1913 550 cc longstroke, it had redesigned timing gear and larger-diameter valves. More particularly, progress had caught up with Triumph in the form of a three-speed gearbox (by Sturmey-Archer) complete with clutch and kick-starter.

This was the celebrated Model H, which was to earn its stripes in the mud of the Flanders battlefields. In the next four years, 20,000 were to be built for the British Army alone, and another 10,000 for the allies. Primary drive was by chain, and final drive by vee-belt, an arrangement that was to survive to the end of the Model H's life.

Not surprisingly, the 550 cc Model H was the backbone of the range when peace returned, followed by the 500 cc TT machine and the two-stroke Junior; to these was added a single-gear version of the Model H, listed as the Model D. But it was soon an open secret that the Coventry concern had under development an all-chain model, with a gearbox of their own make. Its imminent introduction was confirmed when a works-entered sidecar outfit contested the ACU Six Days Trial, based on Llandrindod Wells, in September 1919.

The new model took its place for 1920 as the Model SD, powered by an H-type engine but utilising a frame in which sidecar lugs were included for the first time. The Triumph gearbox was a cross-over pattern, with the chain final drive on the right. As though in celebration of the introduction of a bike intended to haul a chair, the Gloria subsidiary announced a new chassis in which the sidecar wheel was carried on a trailing arm controlled by a volute spring.

The SD stood for Spring Drive, because the clutch of the new gearbox embodied a transmission shock absorber. It comprised a series of radially disposed rollers held in their sockets by a large-diameter coil spring, but able to ride up the socket sides under shock loading.

But Britain was gripped by rocketing inflation and, though the SD was priced at £92 in January 1920, it was around £110 and still rising by March. Similarly, the 225 cc two-stroke shot up from £60 to £72 in the same period.

Meanwhile, the USA had been showing interest in the two-stroke, and Ignatz Schwinn, whose Chicago factory produced the big-twin American Excelsior (and, later, the Henderson four) began to build under licence a copy of the Triumph Junior though with the capacity increased to 269 cc. This was marketed under the Schwinn trade mark and, although the venture was short-lived, it had a curious legacy. Incredibly, the once-familiar fore-and-aft Triumph fork could still be seen, right into the 1970s, on Chicago-built Schwinn bicycles.

The Germans, too, adopted the 269 cc version of the Junior and it was this model, known as the Knirps, that served to restart production at the Nuremberg branch works. In fact, the British and German factories had worked together since 1903. However, in the course of the years the Triumph-

Werke-Nuremberg were to move out of the sphere of the Coventry parent, and by 1929 all ties had been severed. Motor cycle production at TWN survived until 1957, when it was supplanted by typewriter manufacture.

On the home market the Junior continued almost without change until 1923, when it not only became a full two-fifty, but also collected a clutch and kick-starter; a transverse gear lever, across the front of the fuel tank, replaced the handlebar trigger. Retaining belt final drive, and the Triumph rocking front fork, to the very end, it expired at the close of 1925, and was much-loved by everyone who knew it.

In the four-stroke field, the 1921 TT races saw the Triumph factory taking a leap into the future with an engine of such advanced design that it warrants a chapter (14) to itself. This was the Model R. The R was for Ricardo but enthusiasts called it the Riccy.

Chapter 13

The not-so-golden age

VINTAGE ENTHUSIASTS tend to look back to the 1920s as the golden age of motor cycling (and there are even those who insist that history came to a screeching, shuddering stop at the approach of the hungry 1930s). They have a point. Roads were relatively traffic-free, and in choosing a bike for the new season a rider could wade through the catalogues of 100 factories or more.

Motor cycles were still individually built by traditional craftsmen but, with the spread of technological know-how, development was galloping ahead. Belt drive, beaded-edge tyres, flimsy frames and primitive brakes, all in common use at the start of the decade, had disappeared long before the end of it.

However, it is a mistake to consider the industry and sport in isolation. Motor cycling was but a side-show, flanking the major swings and round-abouts of the political and economic scene.

Many thousands of previously static Britons had been introduced during the First World War to mechanised transport. Some became dispatch riders and many more were taught to drive army lorries. With the return of peace they all clamoured for personal powered transport and, with demobilisation gratuity money in their pockets, they were ready to pay for it there and then.

An engineering industry geared for wartime production cannot be immediately switched over to civilian-market manufacture. Redesign and tooling-up take time, but Triumph were more fortunate than many of their pre-war competitors in that their assembly lines had been running full-blast to satisfy government contracts for the Model H, and to continue the same machine for civilian sale was a simple matter.

Or so it might seem but, in fact, a moulders' strike in the iron foundries of Britain dragged on through 1919, keeping the showrooms starved of new bikes. By the time the flow was restored, runaway inflation had pushed prices up and up. The free-spending boom ended as abruptly as it had begun, and prices tumbled down again; industrial unrest was in the air, and the strikes in the coal and rail industries boiled over into the massive General Strike of 1926.

Of the many small motor cycle manufacturers who had launched out with such high hopes in the immediate post-war period, many had perished in the trading slump of 1924, and others lingered on only to sink without trace in the troubled waters of two years later.

Against a background of doleful trading conditions and an all-round shortage of cash, maybe it wasn't surprising that the new lightweight, whipped into the 1923 Triumph range as a last-minute Show surprise, should have about as much impact on the market as a barrel of wet codfish. That was a pity, for the 346 cc (72 × 85 mm) Model LS was, in its own little way, quite brilliant and well ahead of its time.

From a factory that had only recently accepted such startling advances as a gearbox and chain final drive, here was a unit-construction three-speeder with gear primary drive, slipper-type light-alloy piston, all-metal (steel and copper) clutch, and pressure lubrication, from an oscillating plunger pump, to the crankshaft, timing gear and gearbox. Most unusually for a four-stroke design, the engine featured an overhung crank. Also, there were drum brakes on both wheels (something of which not even the Ricardo could boast, in its earlier years).

Yet the LS seemed jinxed from the start. To judge from contemporary reports, even its Show début was overshadowed by substantial price chops affecting its bigger sisters. It was to be a full year before it was seen again—this time, oddly enough, with a dummy-belt-rim rear brake; and, though the selling price was dropped year by year, from an initial £69 to a tempting £39 in its final, 1927, season, the little LS remained an unwanted orphan.

For that matter, customers weren't exactly queueing to put down their money for any other model in the Triumph list. There were still well-breeched enthusiasts around, but with eyes only for the super-sports Ricardo. However, the Priory Street outfit couldn't live on the Riccy alone. They needed a mass-seller, a real bread-and-butter model.

So Siegfried Bettmann took the bold step of asking the Triumph drawing office for a really simple four-stroke, capable of being repaired if necessary in a Barnsley backyard or a Kenya clearing with little more toolkit than a knife and fork. But above all it was to be the two-wheel equivalent of the Model T Ford—a machine that could be sold at the lowest possible price commensurate with a visible level of profit.

The result was the 494 cc Model P, and it wasn't really through shame-facedness that nobody came forward to claim the design credit for it. In truth the Model P was a combined penny-saving exercise carried out under the overall command of works manager Joe Phillips, and some of the methods employed to keep down production costs were rather questionable.

For one thing, the front brake was inherited from the Triumph Model 30 bicycle, and was nothing more than a small-diameter pulley attached to the wheel, with a loop of asbestos rope applying a stranglehold to the pulley as required. Customers asserted that the brake was more effective when the bike was wheeled backward than when it was ridden forward—except in wet weather, when the brake didn't work in either direction.

Potential buyers, too, found rather off-putting the Triumph idea of running the valve stems directly in the iron of the cylinder, instead of in conventional guides. However, the factory did point out that, should wear develop, the cylinder could be sent back to Coventry for guides to be inserted at only nominal charge.

Arranging the multi-storey Priory Street plant for flow production was not easy, but it was achieved, somehow. To keep down the unit cost of bought-out components, an initial build of 20,000 machines was planned, and contracts placed accordingly. The selling price of the Model P was kept a close-guarded secret until the minute before the doors of the London Show of November 1924 were opened, and Triumph salesmen would do no more than smile gently and hint that it would be 'under £50'.

In itself that would have been quite an accomplishment, because the 550 cc Model SD was still listed at £83. But when the placards were put up, there was an absolute sensation. The price was £42 17s 6d, far and away the lowest of any five-hundred yet offered! Indeed, in the months ahead several competitors went bankrupt trying to get down to a similar figure, and famous designer G.H. Jones blamed the fade-out of the oil-cooled Bradshaw engine fairly and squarely on the Model P, with which it hadn't a hope of competing on price.

Notwithstanding the depressed state of the industry in general, orders for the Model P came rolling in, and in the second week of May 1925 the works recorded for the first time a production figure of 1,000 machines. The occasion was celebrated by a tremendous booze-up and wing-ding on the old Triumph sports field at Binley Road, Coventry,

attended by some 5,000 employees, dealers and friends.

Mostly, machines were transported by horse and cart to Coventry station for dispatch by train to the ports and to all parts of Britain, but there were times when the London and North-Western Railway just couldn't cope with the sheer volume (after all, they had to deal not only with Triumph, but with other Coventry factories including Rudge, Coventry-Eagle, Croft-Cameron, Montgomery, Rover, and Francis-Barnett; plus a couple of dozen bicycle makers). A visitor to Priory Street in the heyday of the Model P could well find bikes lined up, awaiting dispatch, along every corridor and in every nook and cranny of the rambling premises.

Export markets were a special target for the Triumph sales force, and the Model P found its way, in ever-increasing numbers, to India, South Africa, Australia, and most other parts of the British Empire. It is on record that over 1,000 machines were imported by Japan.

Buyers lost little time in telling the factory of the Model P's shortcomings (that front brake; a suspect big-end bearing; and a clutch, worked by external scissors-action levers, that was little short of downright lethal), but Triumph were committed to a 20,000 run, come what may, and nothing could be done except note the complaints and put rectification in hand ready for the start of the second 20,000 batch.

The Mark II Model P began to roll off the assembly line late in 1925, and from that point on it settled down to the kind of respectability that Triumph customers had come to expect. Now there were conventional, pressed-in valve guides; the clutch was actuated in the normal way by a thrust rod passing up the bore of the gearbox mainshaft; a caged-roller big-end bearing was employed; and there was an internal-expanding front brake—of a kind.

That front brake looked to be a conventional drum type, but actually it housed a long spring-steel strip, anchored at one end and faced with friction material. 'When the brake is applied,' claimed Triumph literature of the day, 'rotation of the wheels tends to expand the brake harder against the drum, thus giving a powerful yet smooth and progressive braking action.' Today, we would call it semi-servo.

The works still had some Mark I models in stock, and to make room for the redesigned version these were sold to dealers at a heavy discount. By shopping around the showrooms, the thrifty purchaser could get himself a Model P for as little as £35.

With another 6,000-machine batch, production

was to run on through the 1927 season, but now the crest had been passed and not for very many years were Triumph again to reach a 1,000-a-week production target.

To help dispose of the accumulated stocks of bits and pieces, two more models related to the P had been introduced into the range. They were the N (selling at £45, and featuring a heavier type of frame and the oil pump from the TT machine), and the QA, which was really just a Model P with highly polished crankcases and a trendier, Promenade Percy air.

Also for 1927 was a lightweight with the very odd capacity of 277 cc (66.5 × 80 mm), and the explanation of this is that motor cycles in Britain were then taxed by weight, with 220 lb as a demarcation line. The newcomer, listed as the Model W, offered the customer as much engine as possible without stepping above the 200-lb tax limit. The Ricardo soldiered on, but it had received no further development, and now it had been displaced from the top-of-the-range position by a new sportster with a two-valve 498 cc ohv engine evolved by Brooklands record-breaker Vic Horsman.

'They offered me £1,500 for that engine,' recalled Horsman in later years. 'Silly blighters! If only they'd known, I would have given it to them for nothing!'

But the impressive eight-machine 1927 programme was more than Triumph could handle, for the plant was being reorganised for quantity production of a new baby car, the 832 cc Triumph Super Seven. Like the Model P, the car had been the subject of a drawing-office exercise in price-paring and it was listed, in four-seat, open-tourer form, at only £149 10s. Nevertheless, it was the first British light car to feature hydraulic brakes, made by Lockheed.

Accordingly there was a drastic rationalisation of the motor-cycle side, and from the slaughter emerged only four machines with which Triumph faced the 1928 season. These were the 277 cc Model W (pretty much as before), the NP (in essence an updated Model P, but with the price tag held firm at £42 17s 6d), the two-valve TT sportster, and—the only model to depart to any great degree from the previous year's practice—the N de Luxe, graced with a new frame and, for the first time in the firm's history, a saddle tank.

Nor was that all; for fanciers of the marque soon discovered that the long-familiar tank colour scheme of grey and green had been displaced by black tanks having blue side panels on which was displayed a new transfer incorporating a map of the globe.

With the car safely launched, Triumph attention could be switched back to two-wheelers, and the way was prepared for a return to eight models for 1929, of which the newer members were the C-group, comprising the 350 cc ohv (72 × 85 mm) Model CO, the 498 cc sv (80 × 99 mm) Model CN, and the 550 cc sv (84 × 99 mm) Model CSD. Sharing substantially the same crankcase and timing-gear layouts, the C-group trio had the refinement of semi-dry-sump lubrication and, in addition, the three-fifty featured enclosed rockers and pushrods. The CSD, intended as a heavy-duty sidecar haulier, was to find favour with the Automobile Association for patrol duties.

Saddle tanks were standard on all except the unchanged 277 cc Model W, though even there a saddle-tank version, the Model WS, was available at extra cost. A new frame gave the handsome 500 cc ohv super-sportster, now listed as the Model ST, a lower riding position.

Motor cycling was again enjoying a boom, and Triumph production during the year topped the 30,000 mark. Yet it was an Indian summer, and as the vintage years rolled to a close there were hard times ahead. Over in the USA came financial disaster on Wall Street, and the shock waves of the crash were to be felt right round the world—and that included Coventry.

Nevertheless, it was with apparent confidence that Triumph faced the 1930s. Again the range had been thoroughly revised, and it embraced a very attractive unit-construction 175 cc, two-speed two-stroke in a duplex loop frame, and a whole series of overhead-valvers and side-valvers from 250 cc to 550 cc, with inclined engines, full dry-sump oiling and oil reservoirs integral with the crankcase castings. Two bikes, the 550 cc ND de Luxe and a new 493 cc ohv twin-port, the NT, set a high standard of neatness with pressed-steel bonnet covers over crankcase and gearbox.

But it wasn't enough. The depression was biting deeply and, in an almost frantic threshing around to find customers wherever they may be, more and still more models were rushed on to the market. These included a 150 cc two-stroke, supplementing the 175 cc; 'competition' three-fifty and five-hundred singles, complete with upswept exhaust systems and foot-change gearboxes; and, as distinct from the rather average jobs, a couple of classics in the 550 cc sv Model A and 493 cc ohv Model B Silent Scouts, with side panels enclosing the engine, harmonic cams to ensure quiet working, inclined engines with horizontal finning, and oil-bath primary chaincases.

It was at this stage that a lifeline was flung to the distressed motor-cycle industry by the Chancellor

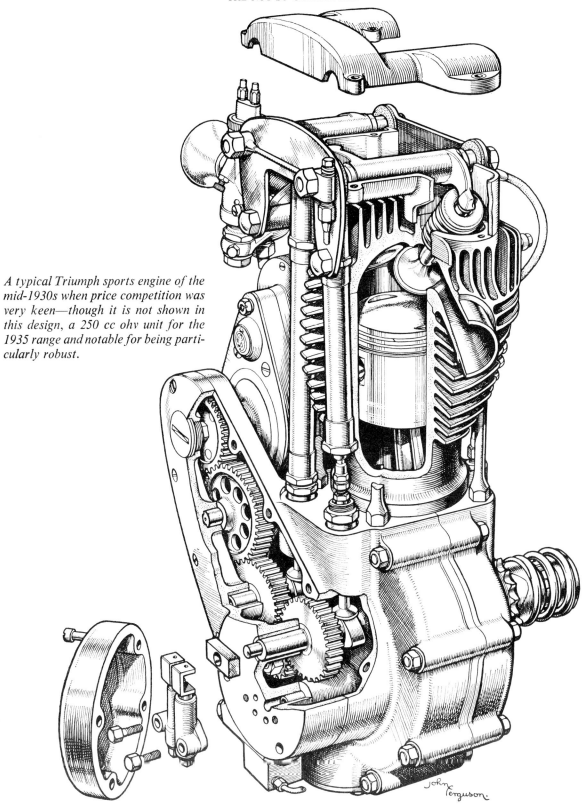

A typical Triumph sports engine of the mid-1930s when price competition was very keen—though it is not shown in this design, a 250 cc ohv unit for the 1935 range and notable for being particularly robust.

John Ferguson.

of the Exchequer, Philip Snowden. In his 1932 Budget he scrapped the old idea of taxation by weight and, in its place, introduced taxation by engine capacity as from January 1 1933, with a bargain rate of only 15s (75p in present currency) a year for 150 cc and under. One effect of this was that designers were no longer restricted to light flywheels, flimsy mudguards and tinplate silencers in an effort to keep within the earlier weight limits. Another effect was a great stampede to get ultra-cheap, under-150 cc models into the shops by January 1.

The main company to benefit from the 15s concession was Villiers, who stepped-up production of their tiny two-stroke engines. Among the new Villiers customers were Triumph, who produced 98 and 150 cc models selling at £16 16s and £21 respectively (and even then they were pipped by Excelsior, who offered a machine powered by the 98 cc Villiers unit for £14 14s).

'The needs of the moment,' the accompanying literature stated, 'call for the most economical and dependable transport. Never has there been a greater need for a low-priced, trouble-free motor cycle, easy to buy, easy to operate, inexpensive to run.'

Perhaps so; but though the rock-bottom cheapies were built at the main Triumph works, the name they bore was that of the subsidiary Gloria concern. Meanwhile, under the direction of A. A. Sykes, the drawing office had been at work on something much better for the 15s-a-year market. This was the 147 cc ohv Model XO, a very lively little inclined-engine mount housed in the duplex loop frame of the earlier two-stroke and, to some degree, an ancestor of the post-war Tiger Cub.

Surprisingly, Triumph now managed to secure from the Ariel factory the services as chief engineer of celebrated designer Val Page, who began work immediately on a galaxy of new machines for 1934 introduction. Top of the range was the 650 cc vertical twin (see Chapter 15) but, in all, there were 18 models, mostly with upright engines. In each capacity class—150, 175, 250, 350 and 500 cc—there was a high-performance version termed the Mark 5, and featuring high-compression piston, high-lift cams, polished cylinder-head ports, foot gear change (except on the one-fifty) and a deep tank in a distinctive finish of plum-colour enamel and chromium plate. There was even, for the following season, a ready-for-the-track 500 cc racer listed as the 5/10, with a specification which gave a super-tuned engine, polished cylinder head and ports, a choice of compression ratios, and either close-ratio or TT-type gear clusters.

All this, though, could not disguise the fact that Triumph were apparently nearing the end of the road. The pushbikes had already gone, Priory Street was closing, and there would be no room at the Foleshill plant for anything other than four-wheelers.

However, as we saw earlier, it didn't happen that way. 'There *will* be Triumphs in 1936 and thereafter,' proclaimed fairy godfather Jack Sangster, waving a magic wand shaped like a cheque book. And there were.

As a postscript, let it be recorded that, in selling off the motor cycles, Triumph Motors—egged on by Lloyds Bank—had dropped the most resounding clanger imaginable. They were to survive as independent car makers for only two more years before, deep in the financial mire, they were hauled out by the helping hand of the Standard Motor Co. As a unit of British Leyland, Standard-Triumph still exists; and the listing, for 1973, of Triumph TR6 models on both two wheels and four was just sheer coincidence!

Chapter 14

The immortal Riccy

THE FOUR-VALVE cylinder-head layout is far from common today, yet it has been around for a long time. There was the Rudge, the early Royal Enfield Bullet, and the British Anzani vee-twin. Above all, there was the Triumph Model R.

The first hint that something was in the air came with the provisional list of entries for the 1921 TT; six places had been booked by the Triumph factory and the wiseacres suddenly took notice.

Mainstay of the existing range was the 550 cc SD, of course, and that was too big for the Senior. Obviously, a new five-hundred was in preparation. But what?

The works had engaged the services of Ricardo and Co Ltd, specialists in piston and combustion-chamber design, commissioning them to evolve something super-sporting within the limits of a fairly tight budget. Frame and cycle parts were to be standard Triumph components, and the Ricardo responsibility mainly began at the crankcase mouth.

Henry Ricardo (later knighted for his services to the motor industry) began by mounting on the crankcase a cylinder with shallow fins machined from a billet of carbon steel, thereby, he claimed, avoiding any chance of distortion owing to uneven wall thickness. Five long studs, nestling in cutaways in the fins, held in place a cylinder head which dispensed with a gasket and, instead, was lapped to make a metal-to-metal joint.

Cast iron was used for the cylinder head. The two pairs of parallel valves were set at 90 degrees to each other, yet the ingenious Ricardo had contrived a combustion chamber as near hemispherical as made no matter. The inlet valve seats were recessed to give the effect of rapid opening and closing of the valves without excessively steep cam flanks. Both inlet valves were served by a common tract, but there were separate exhaust tracts discharging forward parallel to each other. The valve rockers were carried in ball-bearings.

A light-alloy, slipper piston with concave crown was employed and, on the works racers, this was further lightened by drilling so that the piston, complete with gudgeon pin and two narrow rings, weighed only 14 oz.

On trial at Brooklands, the prototype was set to complete one lap flat-out in bottom gear—but that wasn't so drastic as it sounds, because a special two-speed gearbox had been made for the TT, and the bottom ratio was, in fact, 5.6 to 1. Nevertheless, the Riccy returned a 60-mph lap, and the report spoke of 'no sign of distress, the engine remained reasonably cool'.

The rider on that occasion was George Shemans, and the bike was completely equipped with oilbath primary chaincase, silencer, rear stand and, even, a carrier. After an initial series of tests with a Zenith carburettor, it was concluded that an Amac gave better results, and before Ricardo was satisfied another 100 laps of Brooklands were reeled off, at speeds between 65 and 79 mph. On the dynamometer, the engine was producing over 20 bhp which, for those days, was distinctly eyebrow-raising.

Nevertheless, the Coventry works were not putting all their TT eggs in one basket. They had been working on a new, 498 cc racing side-valve unit embodying such developments as a waisted piston, roller cam followers, and the SD-type shock-absorbing clutch. The six race entries were to be divided equally, with Shemans, Charles Sgonina and Stanley Gill handling the trio of Riccy models.

As shipped to the Island, all six bikes had Triumph front forks, but during practice it became obvious that the engines were rather too quick for the old H-type frame, and the machines were dubious handlers. Led by Jack Watson-Bourne, several of the riders demanded—and got—Druid side-spring forks.

In the race, the Ricardos were something of a letdown, with Shemans, in 16th place, the only finisher. On the other hand, the side-valve models turned out to be real flyers, with Fred Edmond making the fastest lap of the race at 56.4 mph before slowing with a split oil tank, and Watson-Bourne running home in fifth berth.

Development continued, and several changes were apparent when the first production version was announced, for the 1922 season. The steel cylinder had been superseded by an iron casting with deeper finning, and the Triumph fork had been replaced by one made under Druid patents. To send the Riccy off in a blaze of glory, Frank Halford—in the course of time to become a very distinguished aircraft designer, and eventually managing director of the De Havilland Engine Co—indulged in a pre-Show spasm of world-record smashing at Brooklands, to take the flying mile at 83.91 mph, the one hour at 76.74 mph and the 50 miles at 77.27 mph.

Earlier, Halford had tried a modified Riccy with an air-cooled cylinder but water-cooled head, the radiator being incorporated in the fore part of the fuel tank; however, the results were not sufficiently encouraging to warrant further experiment.

Ricardo continued his development work and, although the 1922 Senior TT works model looked much as before, it embodied the fruits of a whole winter's labour. Now, the dimensions, formerly 80.9 × 97 mm, were almost square at 85 × 88 mm, and this permitted a 25 per cent increase in valve area. Cams were smaller overall, but wider. The rocker gear, carried, as before, in ball-bearings, was more robust and the exhaust ports were no longer parallel but splayed.

That year, Triumph were pinning their TT hopes on a local 21-year-old, Walter Brandish, son of a Coventry motor-cycle dealer, who had made an impressive début the previous year on a Rover. And Brandish did, indeed, do well, staying to the fore throughout the race, and taking a fine second place at 56.52 mph, despite having no second gear from Signpost Corner on the third of the six laps.

In the usual Triumph way, the TT improvements were incorporated into the next year's production models, and from home and abroad the honours came pouring in. Riccy riders won races in Italy, Belgium and Ceylon, and they scored a one-two-three in the Liège-Paris-Liège marathon. They also collected gold medals in the International Six Days Trial. And, in June 1923, Triumph stood their best-ever chance of winning a Senior TT, for Walter Brandish was on top form and the fastest rider in practice.

But on one fateful morning Brandish came hurtling down from Creg-ny-Baa to find a slower man on his line as he reached the left-hander above Hillberry. He tried to take the dawdler on an outside line, but there just wasn't enough room and he slammed into the banking, breaking a leg. That corner had not previously borne any particular name. It did, from then on!

It could have been that the Ricardo was proving too costly or, maybe, the Coventry factory didn't really fancy the idea of farming out development to an independent outfit. Whatever the reason, Triumph now lost interest in the machine as a racing mount and, instead, switched their efforts to a racer entirely of their own design—an ohv two-valver derived from Victor Horsman's Brooklands job. In the programme, however, the Riccy lingered on until late 1927, but no longer as the queen of the range.

Economic necessity brought a dramatic pruning for 1928, and the Ricardo was not among the four models to survive. Yet in its passing it bequeathed, to the bikes that came after, an heirloom. From 1922 onwards, it had featured a dry-sump lubrication system served by a double-plunger oil pump. That pump, or one looking very much like it, was still keeping the life-blood circulating in the Bonnevilles, Trophies and Daytonas of generations later.

Chapter 15

Premature twins

MOST ENTHUSIASTS think of Triumph twin-cylinder engines only in relation to the classic Edward Turner concept of 1937 onwards. Yet the company's dalliance with the vertical twin had begun long, long before the advent of the Speed Twin. Indeed, the start was around 1909, when Schulte tried the effect of installing a French-built Bercley engine in a Triumph frame.

From those early experiments there evolved the first genuine Triumph vertical twin, even though it appears likely that the designer came from outside the two-wheel industry. Certainly, the engine as announced in August 1913 displayed several light-car features, such as a horizontally split crankcase; it was, said *The Motor Cycle:* 'the embodiment of all that's good in a car engine, but with air-cooled cylinders'.

A 4¼ hp (ie, 600 cc) side-valve, the engine employed a one-piece cylinder block with integral head in which the two exhaust valves were at the front and the two inlet valves at the rear. Very enterprisingly —and pre-dating Honda by over four decades—the crankshaft throws were out of step, the pistons rising and falling alternately. The shaft itself was a one-piece forging, carried on widely separated double-row ball main bearings, and incorporated a large-diameter skew gear in the middle. At the left-hand end of the shaft was a forged-steel, external flywheel, the face of which was drilled then lead-plugged for balancing purposes.

The first Triumph vertical twin, which appeared in 1913. It was of 600 cc and had a cast-iron cylinder block with integral head; the exhaust valves were at the front of the block and the inlets at the rear.

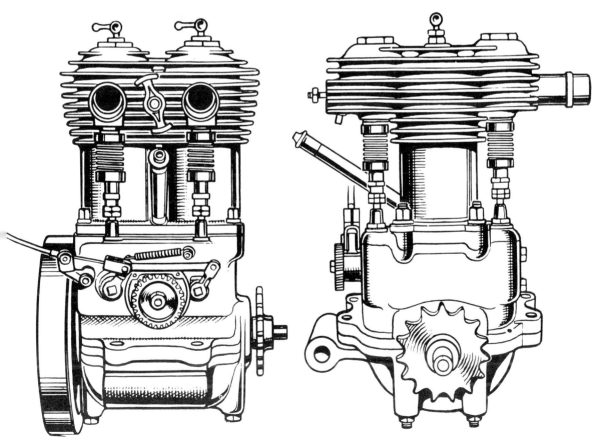

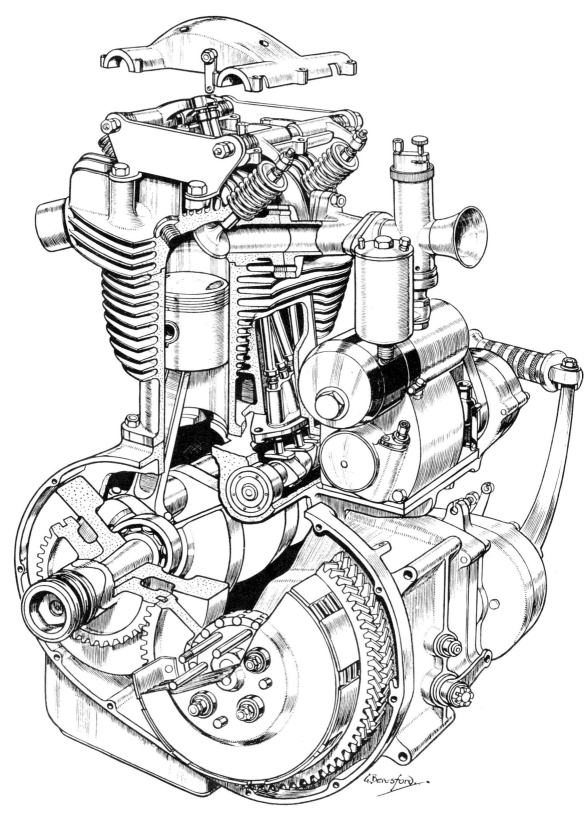

Fore and aft across the middle of the engine was the camshaft, another one-piece component, with two exhaust cams at the front, two inlet cams at the rear, and the necessary skew gear drive in the middle. A further skew gear, on the rear end of the camshaft, drove the magneto.

The engine failed to reach production and, ostensibly, the outbreak of war in 1914 caused its demise. But in the recollections of old-timers, the big problem was vibration.

Some 20 years later a couple of mystery Triumphs, respectively a solo ridden by Syd Slader and a smart sidecar outfit handled by Harry Perrey, slid quietly out of the darkness of an August night to line up alongside other competitors at the conclusion of the 1933 MCC Scarborough Rally. They were the final development prototypes of an entirely new model, the 649 cc (70 × 84 mm) Model 6/1 vertical twin; and they were to return to Coventry that day with a whole sidecar-load of silverware, including the *concours d'élégance* trophy.

Famous Ariel designer Val Page had been recruited to scheme a new range. There were singles of 250, 350 and 500 cc headed by the handsome Mark 5 sportsters (from which, later, Turner's Tiger singles were to evolve). And top of the range was the Model 6/1, a very advanced design with double-helical gear primary drive, semi-unit construction, and a very stiff one-piece crankshaft embodying three bobweights, supplemented by an outside flywheel housed within the cast-light-alloy, oilbath, primary gearcase.

This time the pistons rose and fell together. Driven by a train of gears on the right, a single camshaft lay across the rear of the engine, and the push-rods were inclined forward between the cylinders, as in the later BSA and Norton twins; the camshaft was carried in ball-bearings. Connecting rods were in steel, with white-metal big-end bearings, and the crankpins were each a massive $1\frac{3}{4}$ inches in diameter and $1\frac{1}{4}$ inches long.

Bolted to the rear of the crankcase was a four-speed gearbox and, since there was no intermediate gear in the primary drive, the engine therefore had to 'run backwards'.

Lubrication was dry-sump, with the oil supply carried in an extension of the crankcase, but an un-orthodox aspect of the circulatory system was that the single-plunger oil pump, driven from an eccentric on the camshaft, first delivered the lubricant to an external, pressed-steel filter box at the rear of the gearbox, before it continued circulating round the engine.

Primarily, the Model 6/1 was a sidecar machine, and in consequence the frame was a massive duplex cradle in which the power unit was carried at four points, with a cylinder-head steady bracket in addition. The tapered tubular members of the girder front fork were no less than 1 inch in diameter at their maxima. With externally ribbed, nickel-iron drums, the front and rear brakes were 8 inches in diameter, and interconnected so that the operation of the pedal applied both brakes, while allowing independent front-brake operation from the handlebar lever.

Ingenuity did not end there. Housed at the rear of the primary-drive case was a spring-loaded plunger engaging with a ratchet on the rear brake pedal. This, of course, permitted an outfit to be parked with the brake on; the next operation of the brake pedal disengaged the plunger. Rider features included a quickly detachable rear wheel mounted on taper-roller bearings, and a 28 inch seat height—about an inch higher than was usual for the period. The higher seat was intentional, with the object of improving long-journey comfort.

To match the new twin, there was a special sidecar and chassis (designed by Harry Perrey), in which the smooth contours of the bodywork effectively cloaked the chassis ironwork.

Engineered by Perrey, the Triumph promotional machine went into top gear. Even before the Model 6/1 was announced, the experimental department had chalked up more than 300 miles of high-speed Brooklands lappery, both solo and with sidecar. Following the Scarborough Rally début, Perrey took the prototype outfit through the 1933 International Six Days Trial, earning a gold medal, and then immediately into the 500-miles-in-500 minutes episode described in Chapter 18.

Solid, worthy, and so totally unbreakable that the service department were left virtually unemployed, the big six-fifty ought to have taken the motorcycle world by storm. Certainly it sold, but not in the volume for which the makers had hoped.

At £75 15s, the price was a little on the high side for 1934, but not excessively so. So what was the cause? Weighing-up the machine from a standpoint some 40 years removed, Harry Perrey indicated some of the drawbacks.

'It should have had a foot-change gearbox, right from the start,' he commented. 'By 1934, foot-

Opposite: Modern-style vertical twin, by Val Page, that preceded the Turner Speed Twin by four years. This power unit, the 650 cc Model 6/1, was outstandingly sturdy in design and expensive to produce. The helical-gear primary drive was an unusual refinement on a motor cycle engine.

change gearboxes were well past the experimental stage, yet not until its final year did the Model 6/1 adopt foot-change—and, even then, it was only as an optional extra, an external and rather untidy mechanism grafted on to the top of the box.

'Mainly though, buyers were put off by the sheer bulk of the machine. Carrying oil in the sump made for a tall unit, and we would have done far better to have employed a separate oil tank, so reducing height. When Turner came along with his design a year or two later, he made the engine look smaller than it really was, and people therefore thought it was more manageable.

'Employing two separate camshafts at front and rear of the engine helped Turner to make his unit more comely to look at, but we had a single camshaft at the rear, together with long and whippy push-rods that made the valve gear difficult to quieten. That's about all. Mechanically, it ran like a train and engine trouble was unknown, but if only we had made it look less clumsy it would have been much more acceptable.'

Chapter 16

The military mounts

WHEN THE First World War started in 1914, Triumph were just about to go into production with their best model so far, the 550 cc side-valver with chain primary drive, a Sturmey-Archer three-speed gearbox incorporating a clutch and kick-starter, and belt final drive. Moreover, the sprung front fork, though it had its limitations and was inferior to those fitted by some competitors, had been in production for a decade and was as reliable as the rest of the bike.

Of all the machines used by Britain and her allies in the four-year conflict, the Triumph Model H came out with the best reputation. As mentioned in Chapter 12, around 30,000 machines were supplied on government contracts, and virtually all army riders used them.

It was they who coined the nickname Trusty, which was to become an advertisement line for many years, and in doing so they unconsciously gave Triumph a tremendous boost for the immediate post-war years.

The army boys liked the Model H. It was relatively light and, therefore, easy to manoeuvre and, as often necessary during the winters in Belgium and France, to manhandle. The engine pulled sweetly and powerfully at low revs. With its three-speed gearbox, the bike would easily climb steep hills. Above all, the Model H was reliable and, when maintenance and repairs were necessary, was accessible and easy to work on.

Mauritz Schulte's caution in technical development had paid off. It was said that, from 1907 and the introduction of the 3½ hp models, he had saved the industry from possible extinction when so many machines, launched without being properly developed and tested, were unduly troublesome and fast alienating the market. By the end of the First World War, no other name in motor cycling was as famous as Triumph.

For all except blind optimists, there were years of advance notice of the Second World War, yet no special military motor cycle was ready for production in September 1939.

Inevitably, government supply departments were forced to order listed civilian models, standard except for khaki finish. Machines were accepted from all the major factories, and Triumph contributed the Model 5SW, a no-nonsense, utility job with a 500 cc, side-valve, single-cylinder engine. Its price on the civilian market in September 1939 was £54. A number of three-fifties, 3SWs (price £48 each in 1939), were also supplied.

Meanwhile, Triumph, BSA, Matchless and Royal Enfield were pressing on with prototypes of machines designed to a military specification issued in 1938.

Among the requirements laid down were a capacity over 250 cc and a weight of not more than 250 lb. The three-fifty that Triumph's Edward Turner put forward for evaluation tests, known as the 3TW, had a parallel-twin, ohv engine with the three-speed gearbox in unit, and primary drive by duplex chain.

One of the most interesting features was that the lighting current was supplied by an alternator in the timing chest. This was the first appearance of an alternator on a motor cycle. Later, in post-war years, larger alternators were to supersede entirely the magneto and dynamo on motor cycles; and, later still, the alternator was to become widely adopted on cars.

The 3TW had an unsprung tubular frame (with the fuel tank forming part of the structure) and a girder front fork. Its weight, dry, was 247 lb, just under the limit. The engine's power output was about 17 bhp at 5,400 rpm, and except that the power was produced too high in the rev range— from about 3,000 rpm—the 3TW seemed to be very promising for military work.

Demands by the aircraft industry had meant a shortage of aluminium for other applications and, on later prototypes, cast iron had to be adopted for the cylinder and head of the 3TW; the weight was then up to nearly 260 lb.

But further development work had paid off. The power characteristics had been markedly changed to give plenty of punch at lowish engine revs. Despite having only three speeds, the bike was acclaimed for nippy performance, with excellent steering and general handling. A famous journalist declared it was 'far and away the best Triumph yet produced'.

If the Coventry factory had not been bombed in November 1940, the 3TW might have figured prominently in army equipment.

It was May 1942 before the new factory, at Meriden, was ready. Between times, only limited work could be done in temporary premises in

Warwick. The work included, however, a prototype 500 cc side-valve twin to see how it compared with the three-fifty ohv.

This machine appeared in 1942. The engine—the work of designer Bert Hopwood—had a cylinder block with the valve chests facing forward, and a one-piece head. Both were made in cast iron, but would have been in light alloy had supplies permitted.

The RR56 light-alloy con rods had plain big-end bearings, and the Lo-ex pistons gave a compression ratio of 5 to 1. Unusual for Triumph, the timing gear was chain-driven. Coil ignition and lighting were supplied by a dc dynamo driven at engine speed and incorporating the contact breaker with its reduction gear; it was experimental and known as the dynomatic system. A four-speed gearbox was fitted and, for the first time, a telescopic front fork, giving 5½ inches of movement, was employed.

The whole machine, which weighed 330 lb dry, was intended to be straightforward in design, reliable and easy to maintain and repair.

This machine certainly showed that a side-valve five-hundred twin had possibilities but, when the Meriden factory started production, the new model, known as the 5TW, had to be shelved in favour of keeping up the output of the 3HW, a single-cylinder, ohv three-fifty with only minor changes from the civilian model in the 1939 list. It was this machine which had been built at the temporary factory in Warwick between the end of 1940 and spring of 1942.

All the solo motor cycles for the forces from British factories were, in fact, substantially civilian-type models in khaki finish. But the Ministry of Supply had certainly not abandoned the idea of a specially designed machine that would serve military purposes better.

Manufacturers were given a minimum-requirements specification which included: weight not more than 300 lb; speed, 60 to 70 mph; petrol consumption, 80 mpg at 30 mph; stopping distance, 35 ft from 30 mph; ground clearance, 6 in; and inaudible in use from half a mile.

Edward Turner, then back with Triumph after a brief sojourn at BSA in Birmingham, set about evolving a prototype with his usual zest, and the result was the original TRW.

The engine was the side-valve twin designed earlier but modified in a number of ways, including spur timing gears instead of chain drive. Electrical equipment included an alternator on the drive side of the engine. The telescopic fork was retained.

But the most noticeable innovation was the full enclosure of the rear chain; each run operated in rubberoid tubes connecting the aluminium casting enshrouding the rear sprocket and the rear half of the primary chaincase.

With the war over, the TRW was seen, with prototypes from other factories, at an exhibition of military vehicles in July 1946. At that time, none had been passed for production.

And the necessary sanction proved the stumbling block. As the allied armies were run down, the demand for more machines stopped suddenly. In fact, the British Army was soon to find itself with far more motor cycles in store than it was likely to want in decades.

One-piece casting of cylinder head and rocker boxes on the 350 cc 3TW, the military prototype tested in late 1939.

48: *Demonstrating Triumph's first prototype of a special model, the 3TW, for military use in the Second World War. It is cresting a 1-in-2½ hill on Bagshot Heath, Surrey, in the winter of 1940-41. Total weight was just under the 250 lb set by the WD specification.*

49: *Engine of the 3TW twin. The circular cover on the timing chest gives access to the Lucas alternator supplying the lighting equipment. This was the first appearance of an alternator on a motor-cycle engine and led the way in the development of alternating-current generators which, by the late 1960s, became almost universal on motor cycles and cars.*

50: *Essentials of the first 500 cc twin (the 5TW) for military purposes. It appeared in 1942 and was designed to see if this type of power unit — with side valves — was more suitable for army requirements than the 3TW. One-piece iron castings (iron, owing to the shortage of aluminium alloys) were used for the cylinder head and cylinder block to ensure stiffness.*

51: *The experimental 5TW. Although the engine was new, some of the components were to the specification of the civilian models of the 1939 era. The telescopic front fork, however, was an innovation and seen for the first time on a Triumph. This type of fork was, later, to supersede the girder fork entirely.*

52: *A compromise military model, the TRW. It was sold to governments throughout the world from the late 1940s. Various modifications had been made to the original engine (for instance, spur gears were used, instead of chain, for the camshaft and magneto drives), but the four-speed gearbox, the frame, front fork, wheels and brakes were as for the civilian range of the period. This particular machine is fitted with a compressed-air bottle for quick tyre inflation, competition number plates and other special equipment for the 1949 International Six Days Trial held in Wales; rider was Bill Randall, who finished without any penalties and won a gold medal.*

53: *The illustrious 500 cc TR5 Trophy model, as introduced in 1949 following a magnificent showing in the 1948 ISDT in Italy. With its light weight (aluminium-alloy cylinder head and block) and nippy performance, it became a firm favourite with clubmen as an all-rounder suitable for both competition and road riding.*

54: *By three years later, 1952, the appearance of the Trophy model had been changed markedly by the adoption of orthodox finning for the cylinder block instead of the square finning (which owed its origin to the generator set of the war years) of the earlier model. But none of the endearing characteristics of the first version had been lost.*

55: *The 650 cc 6T Thunderbird of 1950, another world-wide favourite. This model is fitted with the Triumph sprung hub, a neat and ingenious form of springing enclosed in the aluminium-alloy hub shell; later it was made obsolete by the introduction of the pivoted-fork frame. This type of Thunderbird and those that followed it for over 15 years were renowned as docile yet fast long-distance roadsters.*

56: *Three Thunderbirds finish an endurance test at Montlhéry, near Paris, France, to introduce the Thunderbird model with a flourish in September 1949; riders, left to right, are Bob Manns, Len Bayliss and Alex Scobie. The machines each covered 500 miles at an average speed of over 92 mph and finished with a flying lap at over 100 mph — Manns, the fastest, achieved 101.78 mph.*

57: *Bonneville 650 cc T120, the sports version of the Thunderbird, with light-alloy cylinder head and two carburettors. For many years it was one of the fastest six-fifty roadsters available, and had a long list of pro-duction-machine race wins to its credit. This is the 1966 version, with the unit-construction engine and spring frame (in contrast with the sprung hub of the Thunderbird shown on the opposite page).*

58: *Only detail changes are seen in this version of the Bonneville, though it appeared four years later, in 1970. The American influence is seen in the more luxurious dualseat with hand-loop at the rear. Other external differences are air filters, exposed rear-suspension springs, revmeter to match the speedometer, and twin horns on the front tube of the frame.*

59: *The 650 6/1 vertical-twin out-fit at Brooklands in September 1933 after covering 500 miles in under 500 minutes (8 hr 17 m 43 s, 60.28 mph). The feat won the Maudes Trophy for that year. The team is, left to right, Len Crisp, Sid Slader, Tim Robbins, Harry Perrey and, in the sidecar, Bob Holliday, later to become the editor of* Motor Cycling.

60: *Triumph's second Maudes Trophy win, in 1937: Ted Thacker corners his 250 cc model on a wet Donington Park track where the three machines — 250, 350 (Allan Jefferies) and 500 cc (Freddie Clarke) — were run in, after being selected at random from dealers' stocks.*

61: *At Brooklands for the 1937 Maudes Trophy test: Jefferies, Thacker and Clarke respectively on their Tiger 80, 70 and 90 models. Man-in-charge Harry Perrey talks with Clarke.*

62 and 63: *Third Maudes Trophy win for Triumph, February-March 1939: a Speed Twin and a Tiger 100 were ridden from Coventry to John O'Groat's, Land's End and Brooklands track, where they were put through a high-speed test for six hours. On the right, Bill Nicholls (Tiger 100) and Bob Ballard (Speed Twin) are given a send-off from John O'Groat's by Eric Headlam, a sales executive. (Below) Racing-man David Whitworth forcing on the Tiger 100 at Brooklands.*

Motor Catalogue   post free.

Lightweight Motor Cycle, 3 h.p.

PRICE ... ... **£43.**

„ with Magneto... **£50.**

The Triumph Motor Cycle is not an experiment, but an article of proved practical value. It is made throughout in our own works, by experienced workmen only, no female whatever being employed. It embodies many features which experience has taught us give the best results, and, like TRIUMPH Cycles, is

"The best that British workmanship can produce."

Ball bearing crankshaft; M.O. valves; handle-bar control; registered frame; patent cut-out and exhaust valve lifter; powerful band brake; accumulator or magneto; comfortable footrests.

AN EASTER OFFER.

TRIUMPH 2½ H.P. MOTOR,

New and up-to-date Few only left, to clear ... ... **£30.**

Triumph Cycle Company, Limited, Coventry.

ESTABLISHED 1885.

64: *The Triumph advertisement mentioned in Chapter 18.*

The scheme for a special was soft-pedalled, and then shelved on the excuse of being too costly. But Triumph had another card to play. They came up with a hybrid TRW which employed the side-valve twin unit, but otherwise comprised about 80 per cent of components used for the civilian models then (1948-49) in production. In this way the price could be slashed.

This was the final version of the TRW. Although by then it was possible to use light alloy for the cylinder head and block castings, the fitting of a magneto (with an ac generator for lighting only), the four-speed gearbox and other standard equipment had upped the weight to about 40 lb over the specification limit of 300 lb.

Nevertheless, the TRW was a worthy hybrid. Lumbered with so many Ariel, BSA, Matchless, Norton and Royal Enfield single-cylinder bikes of the type that had kept the allies going throughout the war, the Army bought only 12 TRWs! Fortunately, other British military branches, the Marines and the RAF, and armies throughout the world, were less inhibited, and batches of TRWs were built until well into the 1960s.

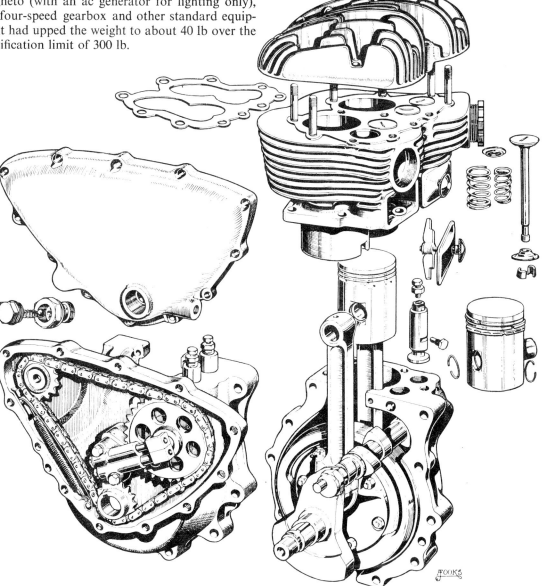

Engine details of the 5TW, a 500 cc side-valve from the drawing board of Bert Hopwood for a special military machine in 1942. It was the basis of the engine for the TRW produced after the war; one of the modifications made was to use spur timing gears instead of a chain drive.

Chapter 17

Favourites

IT BECAME EVIDENT in September 1949 that the Triumph sales department had retained a sense of the dramatic, with the launching of a significant new model from the Edward Turner stable. A 649 cc twin (71 × 82 mm bore and stroke, as compared with the 63 × 80 mm of the five-hundred), it was claimed to develop 34 bhp at 6,000 rpm. And the name, straight from the mythology of the North American Indian, was Thunderbird.

The background to its introduction was a clamour from the fast-expanding United States market for a more powerful machine than the then-current 500 cc twins, capable of sustained high speeds on the vast, smooth highways of that continent. Turner's answer was, in effect, an enlarged Speed Twin. Wherever possible, use was made of Speed Twin components and, superficially, there appeared to be little difference between the two engines.

Introduction of the new machine coincided with a world nickel shortage, which meant that the factory had to keep chromium plating to a minimum. In pre-war and immediate post-war years the fuel tanks had been fully plated, with superimposed top and side panels in colour. Now, Triumph made a virtue of necessity by intimating that the plating process tended to weaken the seam welds and produce leaks; also, the salt air of the sea crossing, combining with the plating salts, encouraged the onset of rust. So the Thunderbird became a trend-setter by adopting a tank painted all over—in steely grey-blue, relieved by chromium-plated styling bands at each side.

The model name, incidentally, had been suggested by Turner himself and was not, as is sometimes supposed, put forward by contacts in the USA. A further interesting sidelight concerns the Ford Thunderbird car, introduced several years after Triumph's motor cycle of the same designation; the Ford company were aware of the motor cycle's existence, and they had the courtesy to ask Triumph for permission before they launched a Thunderbird themselves.

To gain maximum impact for the new bike, the first three production models were taken to Montlhéry Autodrome, on the outskirts of Paris, for a session of high-speed lappery. The arrangements for the test were made by famous pre-war racing men, Tyrell Smith and Ernie Nott, and the riding team comprised Alex Scobie, Len Bayliss, Bob Manns, Allan Jefferies and Jimmy Alves. The official observer on behalf of the ACU was one-legged Harold Taylor (known affectionately as The Colonel in his later years as Britain's moto-cross team manager).

The available fuel was of only 72-octane rating but, on the standard 7-to-1 compression ratio, the Thunderbirds were able to cope. Under a cloudy sky, the session began promptly at 9 am on September 20 1949, when Alex Scobie set out on a couple of warm-up laps, followed in due course by Bob Manns, then Jimmy Alves. Soon the sun had broken through, to highlight the trio of machines circulating consistently at over 90 mph.

Only on No 3 machine was there any trouble when, first, Len Bayliss had to come in to replace a split tank, and then, later, Allan Jefferies had to stop to remove a chain guard that had come loose.

That was all and, after averaging 90 mph for 500 miles (the actual speeds, including stops for re-fuelling, change of riders and, on No 3, time lost in repairs, were 90.30, 90.93, and 86.07 mph) all three machines produced a final flourish with a flying lap each at over 100 mph.

But the Thunderbird was not only speedy. It was also unusually light on fuel for its size—and was to be more economical still with the adoption, for 1952, of an SU carburettor; this change meant modification of the frame seat tube to embody a forged-steel eye through which passed the carburettor intake. Virtually the whole output of the SU Carburettor Co was already committed to the car industry, and the small number of motor-cycle instruments they were able to manufacture were fitted exclusively to Thunderbirds.

Former New Imperial works racer Stan (Ginger) Wood was the SU technician involved in the development of the motor-cycle carburettor, and he came back to the saddle to take part in yet another Triumph publicity exercise in July 1952. His fellow riders were Tyrell Smith, Dennis Hardwicke (at that time Midlands Editor of *Motor Cycling*), Kevin Gover (ditto of *Motor Cycle*) and—surprise, surprise—Edward Turner. In a series of runs over a ten-mile circuit, the test machine returned an astonishing 155 mpg average, at a steady 30 mph.

That year, for the first time, the Thunderbird housed a sealed-beam lamp unit in the familiar fork-top nacelle, and there was a simpler, two-piece fuel-tank construction. But in basic form the model still had a saddle and an unsprung frame, with dual seat and the Triumph sprung-hub rear wheel listed as optional extras.

From Paris came an order for a batch of Thunderbirds for police patrol work, and this was the start of what was to develop later into a special police

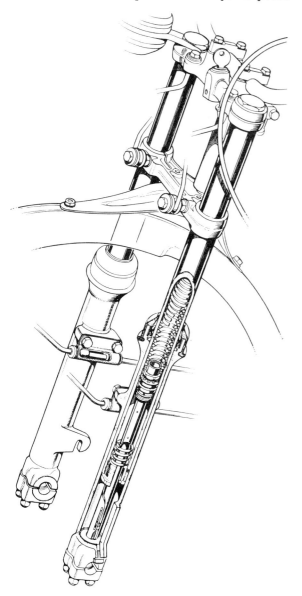

A typical modern telescopic front fork as fitted to Triumphs in the 1970s. The shuttle valves give two-way damping; each one is located at the upper end of the tube attached to each light-alloy leg. The steel stanchion tubes are precision ground and hard-chromium plated; both yokes are steel forgings.

version listed as the 6TP and known, at first unofficially but later officially, as the Saint. The initials, it was said, stood for: Stop Anything In No Time.

For a while the Thunderbird satisfied the power-hungry Americans, but soon it had been ousted from the top of the range by a faster six-fifty, designated the Tiger 110 on which, for 1954, the first pivoted rear fork in this engine capacity was adopted. Next year, the pivoted fork was specified for the Thunderbird, and the days of the sprung hub were over; there was, also, an alternator-supplied electrical system and, adorning the cast-light-alloy primary chaincase, a stylised bird motif, almost identical with that employed later by British Overseas Airways. (Wearers of the Triumph tie, which sported the Thunderbird motif, were occasionally flattered to be mistaken for BOAC pilots!)

As customers transferred their loyalties to the Tiger 110 or Bonneville, so the Thunderbird's share of the market was gradually eroded, yet still it soldiered on. Together with its range-mates it featured, in 1958, the infamous Slickshift gear change (whereby initial movement of the pedal operated the clutch) but, fortunately, this device had gone by 1962.

A duplex frame, 18 inch-diameter wheels and voluminous rear skirting came in 1960. With the replacement of the time-honoured cast-iron cylinder head by a light-alloy pressure die casting for 1961, compression ratio was at last raised from 7 to 1—to the dizzy heights of $7\frac{1}{2}$ to 1!

Unit construction of engine and gearbox came in 1963 and, for the following season, there was a return to a single-down-tube frame (but with a much more robust rear-fork pivot housing than before) and the adoption of a 12-volt electrical system. But by then the sun had long since set on the Thunderbird's day of glory and, by the end of 1966, the model had gone, the last survivor of the nacelle-topped front-fork era.

Probably the most versatile machine ever to carry Triumph tank badges was the 500 cc TR5 Trophy. This was a 1948 London Show surprise and was named in honour of Britain's International Six Days Trial teamsters who, that September in San Remo, Italy, had all but cleared the awards list. To Britain went both the Trophy and the Vase, while the Triumph trio of Allan Jefferies, Jim Alves and Bert Gaymer claimed one of the two manufacturer's team prizes (the other went to Jawa).

Jefferies was the Trophy team captain and Gaymer rode in the Vase trio. For both, and for Alves, the works had devised an extremely light (only 304 lb) little 500 cc twin which was very flexible in its power characteristics.

Based on these specials, the production TR5 Trophy featured a cobby frame of only 53 inch wheelbase, into which was fitted a hybrid power unit of which the lower-end assembly was Tiger 100, apart from softer-profile cams. The square-fin, light-alloy cylinder block came from the Grand Prix racer, but only one carburettor was utilised.

The works trials team helped to promote the popularity of the TR5, and in the next couple of years it earned a tremendous reputation as an all-rounder. Triumph offered various alternatives—camshafts, pistons, gear ratios—and an owner, by dint of a minimum of home tuning, could use the machine for trials, scrambles, clubman road racing or go-to-work riding. At this period in time, motor-cycle sport was by no means the specialised business it was to become in later years, and it was still possible for an enthusiast to ride his Trophy to a meeting, take off the lighting set, go out and win, then ride home again.

For 1951 the cylinder block was changed to a die casting with close-pitch finning. The following year the front fork trail was increased slightly, based on experience of the factory trials team. The weight had dropped to a praiseworthy 295 lb, and the price in Britain was little more than £227, purchase tax included.

But as the 1950s ran their course, so the heyday of the TR5 Trophy passed. Even the works riders had switched to trials Cubs and, with competition hotting-up on every side, there was no longer much call for a general dogsbody of a bike. For 1955 the old, light but unsprung frame had given way to conventional pivoted rear suspension, compression ratios had soared up the scale, and the TR5 was, more and more, taking on the appearance of an American street-scrambler.

Nor was it merely that, for a cuckoo had been hatched in the Triumph nest. The 1957 range included what was ostensibly a 650 cc TR6 Trophy, but in conception it was far removed from the original TR5. Perhaps of neglect, or maybe of a broken heart, the TR5 itself had died before another year had passed. In time the TR6 abandoned all competition pretence and evolved into a single-carburettor version of the Bonneville sports road-ster.

If only the TR5 could have stuck it out until the trail-riding boom of the 1970s arrived; but yet, in a way, the spirit of the original machine was revived. From the chaos that surrounded the dying years of the BSA-Triumph group there emerged a light and attractive little 500 cc job, primarily for off-the-road exploration but good enough, also, for such strenuous usage as demanded by the Royal Signals

Display Team. At first, its name was Trophy Trial; but later on it was tagged Adventurer. In essence, the model was an amalgam of a soft-tuned Tiger 100 power unit and a BSA Victor moto-cross frame. And that, after all, was a fair-enough approximation of the original TR5 concept.

Just occasionally in motor cycling history, enthusiasts have so loved a particular machine that they have awarded it an affectionate diminutive of its catalogue name. There was the Riccy, of course; and others that spring to mind are the Inter (Norton International), the Goldie (BSA Gold Star)—and, inevitably, the Bonnie.

'There is something about the T120,' commented *Motor Cycle*, summing-up a collection of readers' reports. 'Very few motor cyclists could fail to catch that special brand of enthusiasm which clings to the Bonneville as resolutely as does a be-pouched kangaroolet to its mum. The Bonnie owner is he who has taken a deep breath and inhaled oodles of this abundant enthusiasm.'

The name was a salute to those American riders who had, for a number of years, kept the Triumph name well to the forefront at the annual speed sessions staged on the vast Bonneville Salt Flats of Utah, USA. By the autumn of 1958, the Meriden technicians were about to launch a new top-of-the-range 650 cc twin, with sports camshafts, twin car-burettors and a power output of 46 bhp at 6,500 rpm. So when, at Bonneville, Bill Johnson, riding a tuned Tiger 110, achieved a mean flying-mile speed of 147.32 mph, to set a new USA Class C (650 cc stock machine) record, a suitable name for the new-comer was obvious.

Right from the first (1959) season and through the years, the T120 Bonneville has worn neither rear nor midriff enclosure panelling, and its head-lamp was enclosed in a fork-top nacelle for its first year only. It was designed as a super-sports road-ster, pure and simple; that was the way it stayed—and Bonnie-lovers would not have it otherwise.

Naturally, there have been changes in the course of the years. Auto-advance ignition offered a more flexible performance from 1961 onward; a rubber-mounted oil tank from 1962 cured a seam-splitting problem; and, with the coming of Doug Hele to the Meriden development shop, the Bonneville gained vastly improved handling—increased trail, stiffer rear-fork pivot—in addition to adopting unit-con-

Opposite: *Triumph's ultimate in vertical twins, the 750 cc version introduced in mid-1973. Apart from capacity, it is almost identical with the 650 cc Bonne-ville engine. In 1975 a left-side gear-change pedal was introduced to meet USA requirements.*

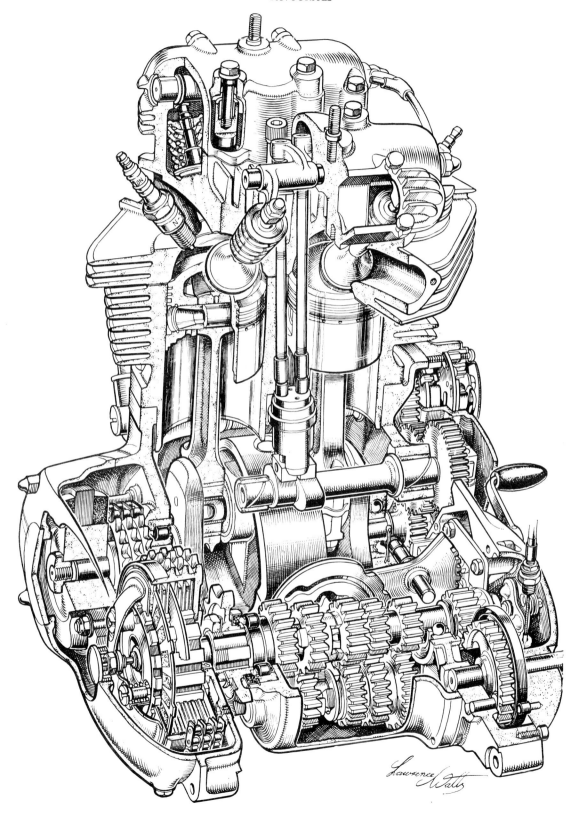

struction of both the engine and gearbox, for 1963.

Over on the other side of the Atlantic, the T120 Bonneville continued to make the running at its spiritual home in Utah. In 1960, for instance, Gary Richards clocked 149.51 mph on an unfaired T120. Then the following year and using the same bike, he upped the figure to 159.54 mph.

In Britain, the growth of production-machine racing found the Bonnie in its element. The 1969 Thruxton 500-mile marathon brought a win at record speed, with other Bonnevilles in second, fifth, sixth and seventh places. But that year the machine reached a peak in its racing career, and thereafter it was to move more and more into the shadow of the Trident.

In company with the single-carburettor TR6 Trophy, the Bonnie underwent considerable re-vamping for 1971. Developed at the BSA group's Umberslade Hall research establishment was a new frame with engine oil carried in its large-diameter tubular spine. A new front fork with fashionably naked upper stanchion tubes was derived from that of the BSA moto-cross machine. And, conveniently overlooking the fact that in Britain, at any rate, the rain fell not mainly on the plain but on the fancy, too, the makers gave it ridiculously short front and rear mudguards.

'An even better Bonneville,' declared Triumph advertising. Not by European standards, it wasn't. Eventually the much-too-high seat height was re-duced by an inch, and customers were given the option of a five-speed gear cluster, but that went only part-way towards rectifying the harm that had been inflicted on the machine's image. Whatever it was, the rehashed bike just wasn't the Bonnie as we had affectionately known it.

Gradually, some of the excesses of Umberslade were eliminated—the headlamp mounted on bent wire, the flimsy front mudguard. And still the Americans demanded more power. They now had

the Trident 750 cc three, but a sizeable slice of the market wanted the less-complicated twin.

In reply, the Bonneville was upped in capacity to 750 cc, but this was not just a matter of boring out the cylinders. The connecting rods were shortened by half an inch, bringing a correspond-ing reduction in cylinder height. The opportunity was taken, also, to redesign the cylinder head and secure it by ten instead of eight studs.

All this, however, took place in the closing months of NVT operations at the Meriden factory, and relatively few of the new 750 cc T140 Bonne-villes (and TR7RV Tigers) reached the showrooms before the works closure plan was announced, sparking off the occupation of the plant by the workforce (see Chapter 5).

The next moves came from the workers them-selves. It was known that impending USA legisla-tion would call for standardisation of motor-cycle controls, with the gear-change pedal on the left and foot-brake pedal on the right. During the months of occupation just such a modification was devised, so that, when production of the Bonnie was at last resumed, the machines were suitable for American market requirements.

In May 1977 an agreement was signed whereby the ties with NVT were severed, and Meriden Motor Cycles Ltd became masters of Triumph destiny. The year, of course, was also the one in which Queen Elizabeth II celebrated her Silver Jubilee, and it was therefore doubly appropriate that Meriden should celebrate its freedom by producing a special Silver Jubilee Bonneville, in limited quantities of 1,000 each for home and export.

Mainly, it was a matter of finish (silver tank and mudguards, with blue panels and red-and-white lining; painted wheel-rim wells; chromium-plated chaincase and timing covers), but these attractive models were welcomed in the market place and sold well.

Chapter 18

Banging the drum

MOST OF US are sceptics and suspicious of advertisements. Mauritz Schulte felt that in the 3 hp model of 1905, powered for the first time by a Triumph engine, the factory had a winner. Advertising declared that it was 'made throughout in our own works by experienced workmen only, no female whatever being employed'. A telling point, perhaps; yet was it enough?

He approached that most celebrated of all journalists, Ixion (Rev Basil H. Davies) who reported later in *Motor Cycle Cavalcade:* 'He was so sure of its merits that he asked me to suggest some stunt that might convince the public. Together we decided that if it could be ridden 200 miles a day for six consecutive days, it would obviously be a good buy for any citizen who desired cheap personal transport.'

Radiating from an Oxford base, the routes ran to Taunton, Derby, Shrewsbury, Ludlow, Grantham and Bournemouth. Douglas Hall, of the Roads Records Association, was booked as official timekeeper, and the period took in the closing days of June 1905.

Triumph provided a magneto-equipped model (£50, compared with the £43 asked for the coil-ignition version) standard in every respect save one. The exception was that it had the first experimental example of the sprung front fork that was to become so familiar in the years ahead. Pivoted at the base of the steering stem, and controlled by a horizontal spring at the top, the fork girder rocked fore-and-aft.

Ixion just couldn't get that prototype fork to function correctly. The original spring was too weak and clashed horribly most of the time, but the replacement was so strong that the bike was virtually unsprung—and that might well have been the root cause of the calamity that befell on Friday, the fifth day of the test, with 1,000 miles covered.

That 1905 three-horse employed a frame with tandem front-down tubes and, when the bike suddenly began to behave like a demented jellyfish, Ixion dismounted to find that both tubes had fractured. Nor was that all. The engine had been losing power steadily, and an examination showed that there had been exceptionally rapid wear of the cylinder and piston rings.

There was nothing that could be done about the engine at that stage, but Schulte decided to build it into a new frame and start the test all over again on the Monday.

This time the test ran to schedule, and by the end of the sixth day 1,279 miles had been logged. But the halted first try was never mentioned in Triumph advertisements; nor was it said that poor Ixion's leg muscles had ached for days from the effort of giving pedal assistance to the failing power unit, that fitting and grinding-in a new exhaust valve was a nightly chore, nor that there had been four stoppages at the roadside to fit new piston rings (one of them scrounged from timekeeper Hall's similar mount).

'I don't know why the piston rings gave trouble,' confessed Schulte, 'but I assure you no Triumph engine has behaved this way before.' There spoke the prototype of every service manager!

Nevertheless, he was always willing to profit from experience. Puzzled by the failure of the valves, piston rings and frame, he engaged a metallurgist, and the outcome was an improved model for 1906, with better materials throughout, a more robust single-down-tube frame, and a developed version of the Triumph sprung fork.

From that point on, the Triumph became recognised as the most reliable motor cycle to date, giving renewed confidence to a public that had begun to spurn the powered two-wheeler as nothing more than an erratic plaything. That year, 500 complete machines were dispatched from the Coventry works and, in addition, engines were shipped to Germany for use in locally built frames at the new branch factory in Bettmann's home town of Nuremberg.

Impressive though it was, Ixion's ride was to be eclipsed totally four years later by the exploits of a Northampton leather merchant, Albert Catt. Riding a 1910 3½ hp model with the Triumph multiplate clutch in the rear hub (though it was still a belt-driven single-speeder), he gave himself the target of 2,000 miles in six days—and, since the period was early November, it meant that his Lucas acetylene headlamp was in use for a fair proportion of the 300-plus miles covered each day.

Douglas Hall was again the official recorder, and Hall's log told a dismal tale of blinding rainstorms near Grantham, snow and sleet at Oxford, ice-

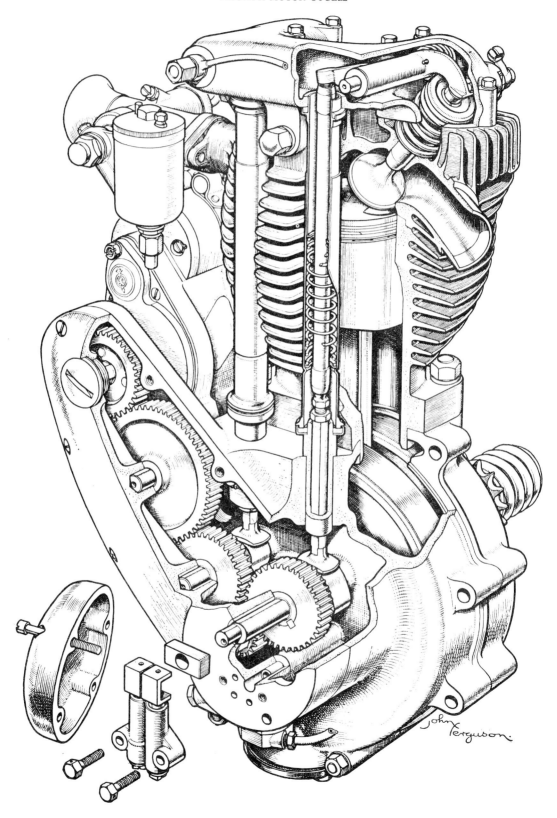

covered roads in North Wales, and fog on the Great North Road.

On the third day, Catt's attempt was almost abandoned through cold and exhaustion. On the fourth, the reckless driver of a pony and trap forced him to take to a ditch. Near Coventry, on the fifth day, he ran into a cart parked broadside across the road without lights, knocking himself out briefly and wiping off a footrest. Yet the 2,000-mile target seemed within reach as he set out from home through the foggy dawn of the sixth day. Then, sharp at 8 am, the engine locked solid on a downgrade near Newmarket.

Stripping off the cylinder, he found the connecting rod immovable on the crankpin but, undaunted, he unbolted the unit from the frame and carried it into the forge of an adjacent flour mill. There, he dismantled it, gripped the con-rod in a vice, and applied white-hot bars to the big-end until it expanded and freed. Then he smoothed the seizure marks with a file (the trouble had been fluff under the oil pump seating, starving the bearings), reassembled the machine and, at an officially noted 2.58 pm, continued his journey.

When he returned to Northampton for the last time, just before midnight, he had covered 1,882½ miles in the six days—and the experience had taken so much out of him that the note of the exhaust rang in his ears for days afterwards. Even so, only six months later Catt completed an even more ambitious programme of 400 miles a day for six days.

How were rides of this nature documented? Catt's Triumph had a Cowey speedometer with mileage-recording drum. Before he set out each morning, timekeeper Hall handed him a packet of pre-stamped postcards addressed to *Motor Cycle*, and from time to time Catt would stop and enter the time, mileage and location on a card. He would have the entries witnessed by some such responsible person as a policeman, postmaster or clergyman, who would than pop the card in the nearest pillar-box.

It was not until after 1923 that publicity rides were brought to a fine art. The manager of the Exeter branch of Maudes Motor Mart, George Pettyt, felt that it would be of genuine value to a potential customer for factory demonstrations to be carried out under strict and impartial observation. To that end, he presented a magnificent trophy to be

awarded by the ACU to the firm staging the most meritorious observed test each year.

Not that Triumph bothered themselves, at first, with the Maudes Trophy (which became something of a Norton monopoly). After all, Vic Horsman's record-breaking rides at Brooklands gave them publicity right through the 1920s.

But 1933 brought to the Triumph camp the motor cycle world's big showman, Harry Perrey. He was a top-line trials rider who was also a first-class salesman with a flair for publicity. He had ridden bikes up Snowdon for BSA, and across the English Channel for Ariel (with a machine on floats). For Triumph, he proposed a Brooklands test of a sidecar outfit, whereby 500 miles would be packed into 500 minutes.

The machine to be used was one of the new Val Page 650 cc vertical twins, hitched to a Gloria sidecar. But, in fact, the idea was even more audacious than it seemed, because, first, Perrey was to ride the outfit through September's International Six Days Trial. This he duly did, losing only five marks and earning a silver medal.

Back at Coventry the machine was stripped and examined; everything was found to be in order and it was reassembled and driven to Brooklands track in Surrey. The weather was foggy, and for three hours following the 8 am start visibility trimmed the average speed to 56 mph. But as the fog lifted so did the pace. With Perrey, Len Crisp and Tim Robbins taking turns in the saddle, and Bob Holliday (author of *Norton Story*, a companion book to this one) and Syd Slader alternating as passengers, the 500-mile mark was reached in 8 hours 17 minutes. With just three minutes in hand, it had been a close call.

The test earned the Maudes Trophy for Triumph. So did the stunt dreamed up and supervised by Harry Perrey in March 1937. This time the plan involved three of the Edward Turner-styled singles: Ted Thacker would ride a 250 cc Tiger 70, Allan Jefferies, a 350 cc Tiger 80; and Freddie Clarke, a 500 cc Tiger 90. Chosen at random by the ACU from dealers' stocks, the machines were to be taken to Donington Park with no preparation other than a routine delivery check. There, after running-in, they would complete a three-hour blast at high speed, to be followed by a maximum-speed lap apiece, at Brooklands.

Sheet ice on the Donington circuit didn't dismay the riders, and the running-in session was completed with only Clarke's five-hundred giving bother—initially a flat rear tyre and, later, grit under an oil-pump seating (shades of Albert Catt, all those years earlier).

Opposite: *The 500 cc Tiger 90 engine as used by Freddie Clarke in the successful Maudes Trophy team of 1937. In standard trim, his machine lapped Brooklands track at over 82 mph.*

It was brighter and warmer for the high-speed work next day and, though Clarke again had oil-pump problems (and had to take to the grass after colliding with Jefferies on the three-fifty), the final reckoning was 79 laps for the two-fifty, 89 for the three-fifty, and 84 for the five-hundred. All that remained was the Brooklands timed lap, in which the trio were clocked respectively at 66.39, 74.68, and 82.31 mph.

So imaginative had Maudes Trophy attempts become that a successful factory might well sit back and say, 'Follow that!'. But Triumph did indeed return to the fray once more, before the outbreak of war silenced the publicists' trumpets.

In March 1939, the ACU selected a 500 cc Speed Twin from the showroom of a Biggleswade dealer, and a Tiger 100 from Sheffield. The two models were checked over at the factory then, with works testers aboard, were set to cover a 1,860-mile journey from Coventry to John O'Groat's, down to Land's End, and on to Brooklands. At the track, racers Ivan Wicksteed and Dave Whitworth would take turns in belting the Tiger 100 around for a six-hour stint, while the familiar team of Jefferies and Clarke would treat the Speed Twin similarly.

Because of snowbound roads in the north of Scotland, the actual route covered was shortened to 1,806 miles, completed at an average speed of 42 mph. At Brooklands, the Tiger 100 returned six hours at 78.5 mph and finished with an 88.46 mph final lap; the Speed Twin's figures were 75.02 mph average and an 84.41 mph last lap. And so utterly reliable had motor cycles become by now that no mechanical trouble whatsoever was encountered—except that the Speed Twin's oil feed to the pressure gauge fractured during the Brooklands lappery and, to save time, the broken end of the pipe was flattened with a hammer to prevent oil loss.

Other factories, too, were making Maudes Trophy attempts that year (including Panther, running a big sloper up and down the Great North Road by day and night), and not until November could the ACU announce that the award was destined, once more, for Coventry. But by that time the black-out shutters had gone up all over Europe, and Triumph had other things to think about.

Chapter 19

ISDT

SINCE THE FIRST International Six Days Trial, in 1913, Triumph machines have taken part in almost every event and won laurels galore, especially from 1948 when, as captain, Allan Jefferies, riding his 500 cc model, led the British team home winners of the major trophy.

Although there are individual awards, the ISDT is essentially a contest between national teams, riders for the International (lately World) Trophy being mounted on home products. Only one team from each nation may compete for the Trophy, but two per nation may be nominated for the International Vase, introduced in 1924, and riders are not restricted to home-produced machines. (The details of these rules were changed for 1975.)

Seven Triumphs were among nearly 160 starters in the first trial of the series, centred on Carlisle in Britain's Lake District, in 1913. Strictly speaking, it was one of a series of Auto-Cycle Union six-day trials, and had been given the accolade of international status by the recently revived world authority, the Fédération Internationale des Clubs Motocyclistes (now known as the Fédération Internationale Motocycliste).

All the Triumphs competed in the 500 cc class and all were still running at the end of the arduous, 780-mile course. They won five gold and two bronze medals. The English team won the International Trophy from France, but no team men were mounted on Triumphs.

Although it was not until 1936 that a Triumph machine helped a British team win—it was the Vase contest that year—every year following the restart of the series in 1920 after the First World War saw Triumph-mounted riders, many of them Continentals, winning individual awards.

The 1948, Jefferies-led Trophy win in Italy had a repercussion in the Triumph range, for his machine was the forerunner of the never-to-be-forgotten TR5 Trophy model. It became a favourite all-round machine for clubmen, who found its versatility a boon; it could be used successfully for trials, scrambles, hill climbs, indeed almost any branch of the sport except top-line road racing, yet was equally at home as a roadster.

There were plenty of other laurels for Triumph in that 1948 ISDT. Jim Alves was a member of Britain's winning Vase team and, along with Jefferies and Bert Gaymer, made up a successful manufacturer's team. It was the first of four consecutive manufacturer's team prizes, 1948 to 1951. And Jim Alves, promoted to the Trophy team, helped Britain win in 1949 and 1950 in Wales riding 500 cc models, and then again in 1951, on a six-fifty, when the location was again in Italy.

In fact, Alves, on 500 and 650 cc models, continued as a Trophy-team member until 1955, riding in Austria, Czechoslovakia and Wales, to bring Britain one win (1953), a second place and two third places. To be chosen to represent Britain in the Trophy team for seven years in succession recognised not only Alves' great ability as a rider but also the merits of his factory Triumphs.

From then on, Triumphs or special machines fitted with Triumph power units have figured in every British Trophy team and, usually, in at least one of the Vase teams. The specials were Cheneys, with frames, forks and other major components purpose-built for ISDT work by Eric Cheney of Fleet, Hants, but Triumph engines and gearboxes were used.

Some riders, such as Johnny Giles, Ken Heanes, Roy Peplow, Eric Chilton and Ray Sayer, were especially prominent during this period, though neither Trophy nor Vase was won by Britain. The Trophy men, though, were very close to victory in 1973, when the trial was held in the United States for the first time in its 60-year history. Arthur Browning, Alan Lampkin, John Pease and Malcolm Rathmell on 500 and 504 cc Triumphs, with Ernie Page and Jim Sandiford riding 125 cc Rickmans, lost four marks to finish second to the mark-free Czechs—the only team of 11 for the Trophy and 14 for the Vase to come through without penalty.

Chapter 20

The racing story

IN THE ANNALS of the Brooklands speed bowl, one particular Triumph holds a unique place. It won a motor-cycle race there, before the track was officially in use!

This odd situation arose because Gordon McMinnies, who became editor of *Motor Cycling* two years later, was in a position to pull a few strings with the circuit owners. Brooklands was due to open in June 1907, but two months before then McMinnies, on a 3½ hp Triumph, was the winner in a one-lap challenge match against Oscar Bickford (5 hp Vindec). His speed was 59.82 mph; and the second decimal place is important, for this was the first recorded use of an electric timing system.

However, the performance of the 3½ hp Triumph was soon to be demonstrated even more effectively. The date was May 28 1907, and, from a starting point alongside the historic Tynwald Mount, on St John's green in the Isle of Man, works riders Jack Marshall and Frank Hulbert pushed their specially prepared machines into life, as first pair away in the first Tourist Trophy meeting.

Showing touching faith in the power and reliability of the engines, the works had dispensed with auxiliary pedalling gear (a point with which Schulte made great play in subsequent letters to the motor cycle press), but the faith was justified. Marshall brought home his machine, at an average speed of 37.11 mph, in second place behind Charlie Collier's Matchless. Hulbert finished third on the other works Triumph.

But that isn't the whole story for, on the third lap of the ten-mile circuit, Marshall had come off near Peel, suffering slight concussion and losing ten minutes before getting under way again. In those early TT races, fuel economy was considered almost as important as outright speed, and it is worth noting that Marshall completed the course at a consumption rate of 114 mpg, and with enough petrol left in the tank to take him another 43 miles.

Overwhelming success came the following year, with Marshall again the hero. He won the single-cylinder class at 40.49 mph, with other Triumph riders in third, fourth, fifth, seventh and tenth positions. Ironically, another 38 years were to pass before a Triumph again took the laurels in an Isle of Man race—the Manx Grand Prix. But it wasn't for the want of trying in that island of speed.

There was, for example, Jack Haswell's second place in the 1912 Senior TT, on a hub-geared model from which the lowest of the three ratios had been extracted, in the interests of more rapid gear-changing between the remaining two. Even more ingenuity was displayed in the 1913 works team machines, where the necessary gear variation was obtained by a Philipson pulley round which a friction band, linked to the rear-brake pedal, was mounted. Application of the brake automatically throttled the pulley down to bottom-gear position—which sounds somewhat disconcerting. Unhappily, that year the factory could claim nothing better than 18th spot.

With the return of peace, the efforts of the race shop at Priory Street were at first directed to the four-valve Ricardo discussed in Chapter 14. Yet though the Riccy was to become the darling of the Promenade Percy set (and, indeed, to chalk up a fair record of track successes) it never did prove itself truly competitive in the Isle of Man.

After 1924, therefore, Triumph gave the Island a miss and, instead, concentrated on developing the two-valver evolved from Vic Horsman's Brooklands racer. It was worth the effort and, after several face-lifts, the TT model was to survive in the production programme until the early 1930s.

In 1927 came the next big Isle of Man push, with machines that looked very similar to the over-the-counter TT Triumphs, except that the works models were dressed in oversize, pannier fuel tanks, finished in grey. Again, the factory seemed jinxed. The bikes just didn't steer properly. Extra frame stays, ending under the footrests, were secured by nuts that hit the road and worked loose when the bike was banked over.

There were seven Triumphs in that 1927 Senior TT line-up, comprising two complete three-man works teams, plus one private owner. To the chagrin of the factory, it was the private owner—Tom Simister, from Birkenhead—who made the best showing by annexing third place. Best of the 'official' riders were Harry Hobbs (an experimental department mileage tester) who was 12th, and a very young Tyrell Smith who followed in 13th position.

It was again Simister who, until a last-lap engine

blow-up at Ballacraine, kept the Triumph name to the fore in 1928. Nevertheless, for real heroism we should single out 19th finisher Harry Hobbs. Earlier in the race he came heavily unstuck, and the machine that he nursed across the line was not much more than a mobile scrapheap—lacking footrests and magneto control lever, and with a dented tank and mudguards, bent handlebar, and a clutch that refused to free.

The firm gave up, and not until six years later was another Triumph seen on the Senior TT grid. By 1934, Val Page was in charge of the design office, and from his handsome Mark 5 super-sports roadster had been evolved a production racer, the Mark 5/10. 'It is confidently expected,' said *Motor Cycle*, at the Mark 5/10's unveiling in April 1934, 'that it will beat the three-figure mark handsomely.'

Triumph thought so, too, and put forward a Senior TT team comprising Tommy Spann, Jock West and Ernie Thomas, with Allan Jefferies in reserve. But so much for expectations, for in preparing the works models a number of clangers were dropped. That year, the machines had a foot-change gearbox, but the locating indentations on the cam-plate edge were not deep enough. It was all too easy to overshoot a gear, with a consequent sudden rise in engine rpm and the likelihood of a dropped-in valve.

Nor was that all. Ernie Thomas reported later that the valve guides were much too short, and gave trouble in the practice period. On one occasion Ernie's piston came up for air—through the front of the cylinder barrel; in the race itself the engine died as he was scooting through Glen Helen and, looking down, he saw that the valve mechanism had disintegrated. None of the team models finished, and the Triumph party returned to Coventry dismayed and disheartened.

Of course, the troubles of the Mark 5/10 were soon rectified, and the bike went on to earn a respectable reputation in private hands. But for Priory Street, it was already too late.

Enter an Irish farmer by the name of Ernie Lyons. Enter, too, the Edward Turner-designed 500 cc Speed Twin, for it was on one of these that Lyons made his Isle of Man début, in the 1938 Senior Manx Grand Prix. It was rather an unhappy début, for he crashed at Cruickshanks Corner, on the exit from Ramsey, and in so doing wrote-off the telephone circuit linking Ramsey to the marshalling posts on the Mountain climb.

Be that as it may, Ernie Lyons was to make his mark in more notable fashion when racing again returned to the Island, in 1946. By now Triumph were at Meriden, and it was there that Brooklands old-timer Freddie Clarke fashioned a remarkable piece of machinery in which the silicon-alloy cylinder head and cylinder block from a wartime airborne generating set (the 'A-squared, P-squared' job) were grafted to the crankcase of a Tiger 100. The front suspension was by one of the new telescopic forks, but the rear wheel was mounted on a prototype sprung hub—patented, but not marketed, by the factory in pre-war times.

First outing for the hybrid was in mid-August, in the Ulster Road Race—they couldn't call it the Ulster Grand Prix at this time—over the famous Clady Circuit. The power output was said to be around 40 bhp, but teething troubles prevented the machine from displaying its true potential.

Today, Ernie Lyons is chairman of a concrete construction firm, but his memories of the immediate post-war racing scene are vivid. The Triumph's problems in the Ulster Road Race, he reports, had a very simple cause, in that, because the carburettor fuel level had been set too low, he used up his supply of racing plugs in a few laps.

'However,' he continues, 'short bursts between plug changes indicated that the bike was a potential winner, so I went to the Island for the Senior Manx Grand Prix full of confidence. There was nothing spectacular about my practice times for a number of reasons, the main one being that in order to spare the machine (for which very few spares were available) I raced only over selected portions of the course, easing back on the straights and as and when I felt I knew particular parts of the course well enough.

'The evening before the Senior, we were jetting the carburettor at Creg-ny-Baa when I noticed what appeared to be a fleck of aluminium on a plug. Everybody present—Fred Clarke, Freddie Dixon and Rex McCandless—assured me that it was nothing to worry about. What they didn't tell me was that they intended stripping the engine, which they did that evening after getting an extension allowing the bike to be weighed in the following morning.

'They apparently worked through a good part of the night and, I believe, lowered the compression ratio. I suspected something was afoot, but I had so much confidence in the people concerned that I did not ask questions. Apart from the engine check-out, they fitted a much longer front mudguard (from my roadster Tiger 100) which was to prove a godsend in the wet.

'When we assembled for the race I was delighted to hear that the weather outlook was doubtful. Curiously enough, I never had any doubts as to

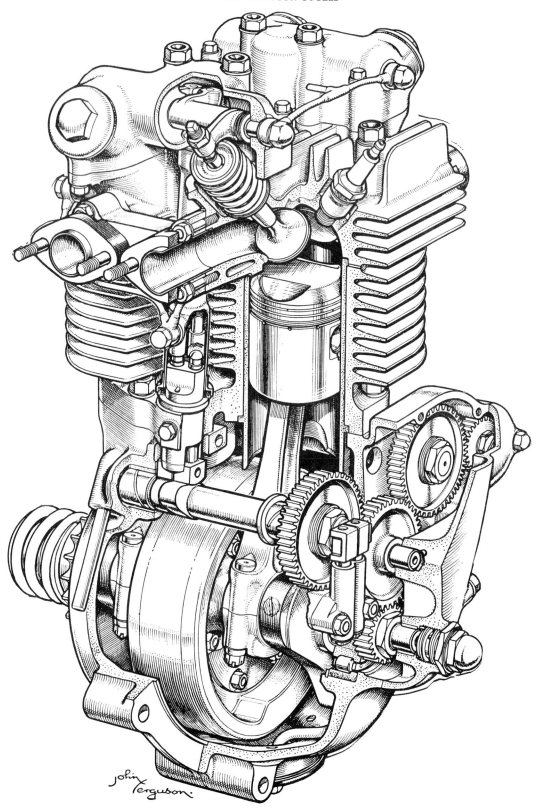

the outcome of the race (no, I didn't have a swollen head; it was just an intuitive feeling) but I knew that I needed wet roads.

'The poor visibility turned out to be an added bonus because, not knowing the Mountain section of the course all that well, I just followed the yellow line and did not bother looking for landmarks to try to decide where I was at any point in time. Another bonus under these conditions was the flexibility of the twin and its relative quietness, which allowed me to hear machines ahead.

'The approaches to Creg-ny-Baa, Hillberry and Signpost remain vividly in my mind. Both at the Creg and Signpost I had to brake long before the corners were visible (I counted slowly from the warning boards approaching these corners), while I had to start peeling off for Hillberry before I could see the bend (a stunted bush, still there, was my marker).

'The last lap was a bit of a nightmare. I tried to slow down, but found I was losing concentration and misjudging corners. After bouncing off a kerb approaching Ramsey, I started racing again and had no further troubles, though towards the end of this lap my revmeter went out of action.

'Oddly enough, though I normally have a poor memory, I can remember every detail of that race. My worst moment was on the second lap when I ran through a pond of rain-water after Ballacraine; the engine cut out, then came in on one and, finally, picked up on two again.

'The race seemed to last a lifetime because it was impossible—as I learned to my cost on the last lap—to relax for one second of time. I doubt if before or since I have ever been so exhausted in any activity. I was soaked through and through, and my goggles tended to fill with water—which had to be tipped out from time to time.

'Curiously, except for the odd moment or two, I enjoyed every minute because of the tremendous challenge involved in the battle against the adverse conditions. This, indeed, was the main motivation because I was on my own for the whole race, apart from passing an occasional rider.'

Lyons led from start to finish, but an inspection of the Triumph in the paddock afterwards revealed that the frame front down tube had broken just above the engine plates. Had the race been longer, the machine would have been a certain retirement.

'I will never know when the frame broke,' concludes Ernie Lyons, 'but it appears to have been responsible for the revmeter going out of action on the last lap. It hardly seems possible that the machine could have covered those last few miles with a broken front down tube, and yet it must have done. Truly, it was a lifetime condensed into one memorable day.'

The Manx success was greeted with terrific enthusiasm by the Triumph-owning public, but Edward Turner's reaction was a grudging one. 'We're certainly not going to go hell-for-leather on a racing programme,' he said, 'though we may be able to offer competitors reasonable support.'

In February 1948, the form of the promised reasonable support was made known by the unveiling of a very handsome motor cycle indeed, the 500 cc Grand Prix. It was the first time since the Mark 5/10 of the mid-1930s that the factory had made a catalogued racer, and its relationship to the Ernie Lyons model was obvious, even to the square-finned cylinder block and hub-sprung rear wheel. All-up weight was a creditable 310 lb.

The Grand Prix was intended as a 'bike for the lads' rather than a title-chaser and, though in the seasons ahead it was to earn a shelf-full of awards in the lesser international meetings, particularly in the hands of David Whitworth, its Isle of Man record was much less happy.

The lower-end assembly was still, basically, that of the sports-roadster Tiger 100, and it was a little unfair, perhaps, to expect it to stand the rigours of long-distance races.

Of the six machines entered for the 1948 Senior TT, every one retired. A year later, 13 examples came to the Senior line and, though fifth and sixth places could be considered reasonable recompense, there were still all too many Triumphs falling by the wayside. By 1950, the Grand Prix was already on its way out. By 1951, with Senior TT entries down to a measly two, it was dead.

Yet the truly great racing days of Triumph were still to come, with the spread of interest in production-machine racing—the sport for which Turner had promised his support so long ago.

It was at Thruxton in Hampshire that the fuse was lit, with the Southampton Club's promotion of a long-distance race for catalogued sports machines, a two-wheel equivalent of the famous Le Mans car race—even to the sprint across the track to get the event under way.

Initially it was a nine-hour race, but in 1958,

Opposite: *The 500 cc Grand Prix engine of 1948 which powered Triumph's production racers of the period. Two years earlier, the prototype—light-alloy cylinder head and block from a wartime generator set grafted on to the lower half of a Tiger 100 unit—had been used by Ernie Lyons to win the Manx Grand Prix.*

under *Motor Cycle* sponsorship, it was revamped to cover a 500-mile distance. In celebration, the major award was won by the formidable pairing of Mike Hailwood and Dan Shorey, taking turns in riding a Triumph 650 cc Tiger 110.

'The race made sense for the first time,' ran the contemporary report, 'in that it was won by a machine of the largest capacity class . . . but it is certainly arguable that Saturday's race was won in the pits—also, that it was won on reliability.'

Reliability; there was that word again! And, as production racing began to catch the public imagination, so Triumph reliability was to pay off time after time. To the *Motor Cycle* 500-miler was added the Hutchinson 100 and then, at last, the first Production Machine TT of 1967—with Triumph Bonnevilles all but monopolising the 750 cc class, and John Hartle (at a 97.1 mph average) making Island history as the first winner of this new type of TT event.

However, if any one man could be said to have made the Production Machine TT his own, it was Welshman Malcolm Uphill, who took a Bonneville twin to a new race record of 99.99 mph in 1969 (twice topping 100 mph for the lap) and then, the following year, repeated the victory, but this time with a three-cylinder 750 cc Triumph Trident.

Percy Tait, Ray Pickrell, Paul Smart, Darryl Pendlebury, Tony Jefferies, Tom Dickie; all played a part in keeping the Triumph name in the racing forefront in the 1970s. But, personalities apart, one particular machine deserves a lasting memorial. Built in the Meriden competitions department as one of three Tridents for the 1970 Production Machine TT works team, it was to collect, in five seasons of racing, 750 cc Production Machine TT races and lap records; it was the first bike to win an Isle of Man production-machine race at over 100 mph; it was twice winner of the Silverstone production event, and a consistent finisher in the Hutchinson 100 and Bol d'Or.

The bike was the near-legendary Slippery Sam (a name bestowed when, after oil-pump failure in a Bol d'Or race, it came home fifth with an oil-plastered exterior). It was the only motor cycle in Island history to have won five TT races in five years. Indeed, Sam contested six Production Machine TT races, but in the first of these, when ridden by Tom Dickie, it finished fourth. However, in 1971 and 1972, in the hands of Ray Pickrell, it was outright winner. In 1973 came its third win, this time for Tony Jefferies, son of Triumph works rider of the 1930s, Allan Jefferies. The fourth victory, in 1974, was by Mick Grant and the

fifth, by Dave Croxford and Alex George in the ten-lap Production TT of 1975, when George hoisted the lap record to 102.88 mph.

In only the first two seasons was Slippery Sam a works-entered model, for the BSA group was running into financial difficulties. The last four wins came when it was privately owned and prepared by Les Williams, of the firm's development department.

Coincidentally with the upsurge in production-machine racing in Europe had come increased interest, in the USA, in the Daytona 200 races. For this prestigious meeting, machines are based on production models, but manufacturers are allowed considerably more latitude in modifications and preparation. However, in this book we are concerned with the American racing picture only as far as it affected the Triumph outlook.

The power unit for the Daytona machines was a 750 cc three-cylinder Trident, but the frame was very different from that of the production model, and in the few years of development work that remained to the Meriden race shop, the Daytona specials begat a potent contender for the new Formula 750 racing class.

It was with an unofficial Brooklands record that we began the chapter, and perhaps it is fitting that we should return to that long-abandoned Surrey venue. As we saw in Chapter 10, when Brooklands closed for ever at the outbreak of war in 1939, three class records were standing to the credit of Triumph riders, and these can, of course, never be broken. One record, the 500 cc, was Wicksteed's, on the blown twin. The other two were set by Freddie Clarke, who joined the Triumph Co in 1937 to help in engine development, and who was to become, first at Priory Street and later at Meriden, chief of the firm's experimental department. At the second Brooklands meeting of 1939, on a dope-burning Tiger 80 equipped with a small sprint tank, he raised the 350 cc lap record to an all-time 105.97 mph. Then, at the end of June, he appeared on an unusual model for an unusual reason.

It was a 500 cc Tiger 100 twin, bored out by 0.01 inch in each cylinder to give a capacity of 503 cc so that Freddie, on a works model, would not be in direct competition with Triumph-owning privateers. In Clarke's own words, for the first time he was in possession of a machine with a performance far in excess of the handicapper's estimate, and the outcome was two race wins and the raising of the 750 cc-class lap record to 118.02 mph—precisely the speed achieved by Ivan Wicksteed, on the supercharged twin, in setting the 500 cc record.

65: *A picture that epitomises the International Six Days Trial: Dutch rider B. H. Olie, on a 650 cc Triumph, floods German rider behind, H. Oelerich (350 Victoria), at the Diluw river during the 1954 event in Wales.*

66: *Jim Alves, one of Triumph's greatest trials exponents, especially in ISDTs. Here he is about to start one of the day's routes in Czechoslovakia in 1953, when he was a member of Britain's winning Trophy team.*

67: *Ken Heanes, famous Triumph rider and in recent years Britain's team manager, during the 1966 ISDT, held in Sweden.*

68: *(Below) A line-up of special Cheney machines, with Triumph engines and gearboxes, ready for the 1970 ISDT.*

69: *Jack Marshall, following up his second place in the single-cylinder class of the first TT race in the Isle of Man, 1907, leads the way home in 1908 with a fine win at 40.49 mph for the 158 miles. He made the fastest lap also, with a speed of 42.48 mph.*

70: *A very early high-speed Triumph — the 3½ hp Model TT of 1912, single-speed with direct belt drive from engine pulley to the rear wheel, stripped for racing at Brooklands track.*

71: (*Below*) *The Triumph for the 1926 Senior TT fitted with the two-valve engine developed by Victor Horsman. Interestingly, it is equipped with a positive-stop* hand *change for the three-speed gearbox.*

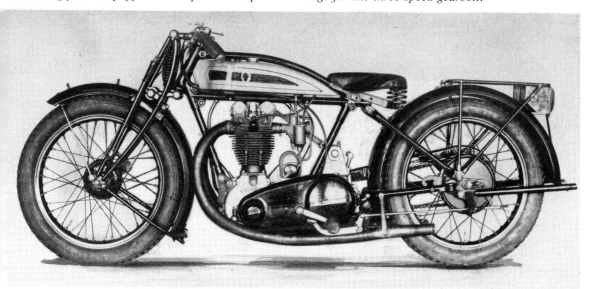

72: *A famous win: Ernie Lyons, from Ireland, on his way to heading the field home in the 1946 Senior Manx Grand Prix. His 500 cc Triumph was the prototype of the Grand Prix model.*

73: *David Whitworth, a consistent campaigner on a GP Triumph in the major continental road races in 1947, cornering in the Dutch TT.*

74: *Famous American rider, Gary Nixon, in his homeland's biggest race, the Daytona 200, in 1971. He rides the race-kitted three-cylinder Trident.*

75: *Mike Hailwood, among the all-time greats of road racing, rides a Tiger 110 to victory in the Thruxton 500-mile production-machine race in 1958; his co-rider was Dan Shorey.*

76: *A 1972 shot of Ray Pickrell winning the 750 cc class of the Production TT on a Trident (Slippery Sam) at a speed of 100 mph. That year, Trident-mounted again, he also won the Formula 750 race, at 104.23 mph. In addition, he set lap records of 101.61 mph and 105.68 mph respectively.*

77: *The Edward Turner-designed 350 cc double-ohc Bandit SS of 1971. It never reached the production stage.*

78: *Designer Val Page.*

79: *Designer Bert Hopwood.*

80: *Engineer Doug Hele.*

81: *Allan Jefferies on the side-valve Triumph climbs Breakheart Hill on his way to winning the 1938 British Experts' Trial.*

82: *Jack Marshall.* **83:** *Victor Horsman.* **84:** *Tom Simister.* **85:** *Jim Alves.* **86:** *Roy Peplow.*

87: *Ken Heanes.* **88:** *Percy Tait.* **89:** *Ray Pickrell.* **90:** *Tony Jefferies.* **91:** *Paul Smart.*

Chapter 21

The technicians

THOUGH THE OPENING years of the twentieth century saw, in Britain, a dawning interest in the powered two-wheeler, the majority of the machines on offer were crude, unwieldy and unreliable. The spark of enthusiasm, it seemed, would be quenched before it had a chance to spurt into flame.

But Ixion of *The Motor Cycle* was to identify two factors that, in his view, saved the sport from premature collapse. One was the invention of the high-tension magneto; the other was the steadfastness of **Mauritz Schulte**, managing director of Triumph, whose interest in motor cycles dated from his personal experience with an 1895 Hildebrand and Wolfmuller.

Just as Bettmann was the business genius behind Triumph's early progress, so was Mauritz Schulte the architect of Triumph's technical superiority over rival makes. He was not a designer in the currently accepted sense—drawing-board work was left to his works manager, Charles Hathaway—but he saw that what was needed to restore public confidence was a simple but rugged machine, built of the best materials available by first-class craftsmen.

In that respect the 1905 'three-horse', the first Triumph to boast an engine of the firm's own manufacture, was as much Schulte's brain-child as it was Hathaway's. Nor was it just design, for Schulte maintained rigid control of quality through every stage of its building, and it was this that gave the 3 hp its reputation for sterling performance and unfailing reliability.

The picture that comes through to us is of a man conservative by nature, who would study any suggested modification from every aspect, never allowing himself to be rushed into hasty action. His conscience would not allow him to market anything of which he was not completely sure, and many were the novelties (such as a two-speed epicyclic rear hub in conjunction with an engine-shaft clutch) tested in secret—often with the connivance of Ixion—only to be set aside as unworthy of carrying the Triumph name.

Bettmann, on the other hand, appears to have been rather more mercurial in temperament and, though their partnership was to last for many years, it was inevitable that the break-up would come sooner or later. Said Bettmann: 'My relationship with Schulte, as is usually the case when two opposite characters have to work together, became at last somewhat strained'.

Schulte's departure from Triumph came in 1919 and, unhappily, he died only two or three years later.

For the next decade, Triumph held and, indeed, extended its position in the motor-cycle field but, as the 1920s faded into the grey 1930s, so the factory, by then heavily embroiled in car production, reached semi-stagnation on the two-wheeler side. Certainly there were some exceptions, such as a lively little overhead-valve 250 cc, but the rest could be classed as worthy but unremarkable.

At that point **Val Page** was engaged as chief designer, commissioned to scheme a completely new range. London born, Valentine Page had evolved his first motor cycle (with a Fafnir engine housed in a home-built frame with Chater-Lea fittings) as far back as 1908, while serving an apprenticeship with a southern motor agency. By 1914 he had moved to the drawing office of J. A. Prestwich, the renowned proprietary-engine builders.

At the JAP works, Val Page became more and more involved in the design of racing engines, and much of his time was spent at Brooklands in the company of such stars of the day as Sid Moram and Bert Le Vack. From his board came a double-overhead-camshaft three-fifty with which Le Vack, in 1922, recorded 91.88 mph for the flying mile. Later, Page produced a 1,000 cc vee-twin, which gained the world five-mile record.

Meanwhile the Ariel works at Selly Oak, after flirtation with car manufacture, had decided to abandon the four-wheelers and revitalise its motor cycle production. Val Page was lured away from London in 1925, and offered a free hand to produce a completely new Ariel image. That he certainly did, and the Page-inspired Ariels of the later 1920s took that company right into the forefront.

With the collapse of the original Ariel firm in 1932, Page moved his drawing board south to Triumph's Priory Street works, there to begin work on a whole new family of models for 1934 introduction. In the range as unveiled at the 1933 Olympia Show there were no fewer than 18 models, based on three frame sizes and extending from an inclined-engine 147 cc single, to Page's masterpiece, the 650 cc vertical twin.

Of course, not all the machines were his responsibility. The vertical-engine side-valve and overhead-valve models from 250 cc upward certainly were though, and to some extent they exhibited an Ariel parentage. In each capacity class (even the one-fifty) there was a de luxe version listed as the Mark 5, and this indicated polished cylinder-head ports, higher compression ratios, stronger valve springs, polished Birmabright primary chaincase and—except on the one-fifty—foot-change gear operation. The identification point of the Mark 5 series was a chromium-plated fuel tank with plum-coloured side panels.

Back at Selly Oak, Page had worked with Edward Turner when the latter was engaged by Jack Sangster to develop the Square Four. But when, in 1936, the Triumph plant changed hands and Turner was put in overall control it was time for Page to move on again — at first to BSA (where the Ariel and then Triumph family likeness could be traced in his new designs, including the M20 and Gold Star); finally, he went back to Ariel for the KH twin and, his swan song, the 250 cc twin two-stroke Leader.

Courteous and gentlemanly in manner, scholarly in appearance, Val Page was an unlikely character to find in a motor-cycle design office. But on his record he must surely be counted as one of the most outstanding designers the industry has produced.

London was also the birthplace of the next man to occupy the chief designer's desk at Priory Street, **Edward Turner.** But now it was 1936 and, under the Triumph Engineering Co banner, Turner doubled as designer and general manager.

A radio operator in the Merchant Navy at the age of 14, he had opened his own motor-cycle shop in Dulwich, south London, in the mid-1920s. There he became a manufacturer in his own right, with the announcement (in January 1927) of the 350 cc face-cam Turner Special, selling at £75.

That bike brought Turner to the attention of Jack Sangster, and Sangster became more interested still when he learned of Turner's plans for a four-cylinder machine in which the cylinders, in a block casting, would be arranged as two pairs of parallel twins. And so Turner went to Selly Oak to develop the machine that the world was to know as the Ariel Square Four—and, incidentally, to continue Page's work on the Ariel Red Hunter singles.

A determined and ambitious man who had no time for fools, he was to bring a kind of engineering

dictatorship to Triumph but, of course, it was the right policy for the situation in which the firm had found itself. Above all, though, Edward Turner had a flair for styling, and this was soon evident in the minor touches which, when applied to Val Page's Mark 5 sportsters, transformed them into the best-selling Tiger singles.

Obviously, the pre-Turner range of 18 or more Triumphs had to be rationalised, and one of the first moves was to trim the list to two types of frame, two types of front fork, and one basic gearbox. In all the hubbub of making the products viable and getting the factory back into production, it seemed barely possible that Turner would have time for any original design work. And yet it was at this stage that he created the machine that changed the whole concept of motor-cycle design —the Speed Twin.

For all his undoubted ability, Turner was never an easy man to work with, and it was a clash of personalities that led to his departure from Triumph in 1942. His destination was BSA; but before very long the differences had been patched up, and he returned to Triumph with even more authority—as managing director.

The designs of the later Turner period included a new lightweight single, the 150 cc Terrier (soon to grow into the 200 cc Tiger Cub). There was an uneasy venture into scooterdom with the 250 cc vertical-twin Tigress. Also, the motor cycle twins adopted unit construction. But the BSA-Triumph merger gave Edward Turner more scope, and his projects were to embrace car engines such as the Daimler SP250 V-8, and Majestic Major, the valve geometry of which was adapted from Triumph Thunderbird practice.

Though he was to retire from Meriden in 1964, Turner maintained his interest in motor-cycle design, and it was as a freelance that he carried through to prototype stage the last Turner project of all. This was a light and compact 350 cc twin, with twin overhead camshafts, and in preliminary tests at the MIRA proving circuit it was reputed to have achieved over 110 mph.

The design was bought for production and, after a few modifications to the original layout, was announced as the Triumph Bandit (or, in a different style of painting, the BSA Fury). Half-a-dozen examples were constructed in the tool room but, by this time, BSA-Triumph were on the downward slope, and development problems caused the Bandit to be put aside.

Turner had not been in the best of health for some years, and in 1973, at the age of 72, he died at his Dorking home following a coronary thrombosis.

Val Page, Edward Turner . . . and there had been a third occupant of that Ariel drawing office of the early 1930s. He was **Bert Hopwood,** Birmingham born and bred, who had begun his engineering career in traditional fashion, as tea-boy in the Ariel foundry. As Hopwood's apprenticeship continued, so he progressed through every branch of motor-cycle manufacture and, eventually, the path led to the drawing office.

There, as a junior, he was Val Page's assistant. Later, he was allocated to Edward Turner to help in making the detail drawings of the Square Four. In the reconstruction of the Ariel firm in 1932, Hopwood became chief draughtsman and when, four years later, Turner was put in command at Triumph, Hopwood accompanied him as design assistant; in that capacity, he was involved in detail work on the Speed Twin and Tiger 100.

Bert Hopwood stayed with the Triumph company through the war period but, in 1947, there came an attractive offer from the Norton factory. There, as chief designer, the immediate task was the updating of the existing range, and the plotting of a new gearbox. But soon he was at work on the first engine for which he could assume entire responsibility. It was the 500 cc Norton Dominator vertical twin; it was to sire a family of which the latest representative is the Commando.

Hopwood's stay at Bracebridge Street was relatively short. Within two years he was working at BSA on the modernisation of the Gold Star sports singles, and the engine that was to achieve near-immortality as the A10 Golden Flash six-fifty. By 1955 he was chief engineer of the BSA group but, by the following year, he had returned to Norton as director, technical manager, and production chief.

Working with Hopwood at Bracebridge Street as development engineer was another Birmingham native, **Doug Hele.** He was to hit the headlines in 1961 as the man who produced the road-racing twin (the Norton Domiracer) that Tom Phillis had piloted into a heart-lifting third place in the Senior TT.

So well did Bert and Doug operate in double harness that, when Bert took over the Meriden reins from Edward Turner, he invited Doug to assume the responsibility of Triumph development engineer and race-shop chief.

From that partnership came the three-cylinder Trident. And from Doug Hele's enthusiast-manned racing department came the Triumphs—twins and triples—that were to carry the Meriden image to new heights at Daytona, Silverstone, Thruxton, the Isle of Man, and anywhere else that a well-tuned but basically roadster model could demonstrate its prowess.

On the collapse of BSA-Triumph, the Norton Villiers group staged a salvage operation involving a near-£10 million investment. It was, said the wags, a mighty expensive way of bringing Doug Hele back into the Norton fold. But worth it!

Chapter 22

The Yorkshire Flyer

SELECTING A TEAM to represent a nation in the International Six Days Trial is, of course, a very serious business. First, there is a short-list to be drawn up. Then, so that a final selection can be made, the nominated men are put through their paces, against the clock, over similar territory to that of the trial itself.

Yet the ability to ride a motor cycle along rough tracks to a tight time schedule is not, in itself, enough. The ideal team man must be able to deal with minor mechanical failures or tyre troubles, and still clock-in at the next control point within his time allowance.

So the selection committee tend to lurk around corners somewhere along the route, ready to stop a man in full flight and order him to renew a throttle slide, or change a clutch cable, while they consult their stopwatches.

All of which explains why British ISDT team aspirants, charging across the wild Welsh countryside during the 1938 selection tests, found themselves halted and told to change their front tyres. To the general consternation of officialdom, Triumph-mounted Allan Jefferies just gave a broad, slow grin, reached into a pocket and produced his tyre-changing kit—one spanner and a pair of pliers. Yet with those unlikely looking tools he had the wheel out, and the tyre off and on again, in a shorter time than any of the others.

The incident was typical of the tall, practical joker from Shipley who became known, to a generation and more of enthusiasts, as the 'Yorkshire Flyer'. An all-rounder whose competitive career took in trials, scrambles, road racing and, somewhere along the way, a spell as a speedway mechanic to the greatest names of the day, Allan Jefferies won his first ISDT gold medal, on a Scott, in 1928. Captain of the British ISDT Trophy team, and riding a Triumph twin of which the front-fork damping had, by the last day, completely disappeared, he won his last gold medal 20 years later, in 1948.

To explain his dexterity with tyres, we must go back to 1921, when a 16-year-old Allan was sent off from his Shipley home to begin work in a Bradford accountant's office.

'I looked in,' says he, 'saw nobody about and went home again. That was the beginning and end of my career as an accountant. Instead, I told my father I wanted to work in the family garage business, so he took me on, at half-a-crown a week. I did the most menial jobs about the place, principally tyre changing and repairs.

'There were no such things as air lines or compressors. Every tyre had to be blown up with a hand pump. Not only that, but beaded-edge car tyres needed something like 80 psi pressure. That's why, when I rode in ISDTs in later years, nobody could live with me when it came to swopping tyres!'

Both cars and motor cycles were sold at the Jefferies business which stood (as it does today) almost within sight of the Scott motor-cycle works in Shipley. But Jefferies senior had no interest in motor-cycle sport, nor would he allow young Allan to have a bike of his own.

Nevertheless, it was part of Allan's duties to nip down to the Scott factory to collect spares and there, naturally, he could worship such famous works riders as Clarry Wood, Harry Langman and Tim Wood. 'Hello, young Jefferies,' said the Scott spares manager on one such visit in 1923. 'Going to have a go in our trial? Here's an entry form!'

The Scott Trial was, and is, none of your tin-pot trickles up a bank and round a couple of bushes. It was, and is, a full-blooded scramble across the juiciest and rockiest stretches of Yorkshire moorland available; but Allan wasn't going to tell his father that, and he gained reluctant permission to ride a borrowed Triumph Ricardo 'because my pal wanted me to try it out in a local reliability trial'. Great emphasis was laid on the 'reliability' part . . .

'Back around Easter,' continues Allan, 'we had sold that Ricardo to a pal of mine who agreed to lend it to me for the day. Mind you, I had never ridden in any kind of competition before and, in the event, I had to nip off and run alongside on anything more than a 1-in-40 slope, because the back tyre was almost bald.'

He sought advice from the Scott crowd, too, and they told him that riding would be hot work, so it would be unwise to wear too many clothes. He came to the line wearing ordinary slacks—and patent-leather shoes!

'I had no overtrousers, and after one watersplash I was soaked right up to the thighs. Then my wet knee came into contact with the exposed terminal of the Triumph's sparking plug and I must have broken the world's record for the sitting high jump.

'At the lunch break, somebody gave me a glass of what I thought was lemonade. I gulped it down and found it was whisky, so my recollection of the afternoon part of the run is a bit hazy. I know I didn't finish, anyway . . .'

The shoes didn't retain their shine for long or, for that matter, their shape. And because the regulations had said, in big print 'this is not a race', he was very surprised to be passed at great speed by so many competitors. The other riders, he concluded, had not read the regulations as carefully as he had done. Still, his reasons for failing to complete the course were more mechanical than alcoholic, and the Ricardo expired with broken kickstarter, broken exhaust-valve lifter and, finally, a non-operative clutch.

Incredibly, the same friend lent him a Norton for the next year's Leeds £200 Trial—an event that was to be a turning point in Allan's life. Harry Langman had drawn the next riding number to young Jefferies, and Harry was so amused by Allan's struggles that they palled up. The outcome was the loan of a works Scott for the 1925 Scott Trial—'because,' says Allan, 'Harry reckoned he owed me something as payment for the entertainment!'

On a succession of borrowed bikes, Allan made lurching progress through the trials and scrambles scene. Then, for the 1928 ISDT (based that year at Harrogate) came yet another works Scott on loan. Even then, Allan was a trifle green in the ways of trials men and, with a mixture of pride and innocence, he put down 'works rider' on the entry form. 'That honesty cost me another £7 in entry fees, and brought a lot of laughs at my expense. I learned a whole lot after that.'

Soon afterwards he teamed up with speedway rider (and later, promoter) Frank Varey, servicing Varey's and Max Grosskreutz's machines at Belle Vue Stadium. There followed a trip with Frank Varey and Sprouts Elder to the Argentine—and, incidentally, for Allan himself a first venture into road racing, with third place (on an AJS) in the Argentine Grand Prix.

'The Ajay,' he says, 'was running on wood alcohol, and that gradually dissolved the rubber pipe linking the two halves of the tank. I must have stopped a dozen times in the race to clean out the carburettor.'

The speedway interlude was over by 1933, in the same year as the famous tie-in with Triumph. At the Olympia Show, Allan got into conversation with Triumph sales and competitions manager,

Harry Perrey, and the sequel was a Triumph contract.

Next season, on Coventry-built machines, he was runner-up in the Scott Trial, won awards in 15 other one-day events, plus the Scottish Six Days Trial and the ISDT—and qualified as a reserve for the 1934 Senior TT, on a works-entered Mark 5/10. That racer still exists, in the possession of Vintage MCC member John Joiner; and at the time of writing it still displays the dents in the fuel tank and exhaust pipe, received when Allan dropped it one practice morning at the Gooseneck.

'But I have never really counted myself as a road racer,' says Jefferies, 'and though I did qualify for the TT, it was not until after the war that I had the chance of a real bash on the TT course.'

That chance came with the introduction of the ACU Clubman's TT in 1947, when Allan, on a fully equipped roadster Tiger 100, finished second to Eric Briggs (Norton). The following year he retired with a split tank; and the year after—his last as an active competitor—he was second again in the 500 cc class, this time to a lad making his TT racing début, one Geoff Duke.

It was back in the tight little world of one-day trials that Allan Jefferies was to bring off the biggest sensation of his whole career. On a home-brewed, 500 cc side-valve Triumph, he had a shock win in the 1938 British Experts' Trial, the one-and-only occasion in the history of the exclusive event that victory had gone to a machine of that type. Three weeks earlier, he had had the audacity to ride the same machine in the Scott Trial.

'Why a side-valve? Oh, I don't know,' answers Allan. 'It was the sort of daft thing I did in those days, but it was all my own idea and nothing to do with the works.

'Triumph had been making a dead loss of a 350 cc side-valve which, by my reckoning, didn't work well because the valves were too big. Now, if I were to enlarge that engine to a five-hundred, keeping the valve diameters unchanged, the breathing ought to be about right. In much the same way, squeezing the crankshaft assembly of the 500 cc 5S side-valve into the three-fifty crankcase should produce a light and compact unit.

'But it wasn't so straightforward as all that because, although the five-hundred flywheels would fit into the three-fifty crankcase—just about—there was then barely enough room for oil, and it kept aerating.

'I had been hoping to use the machine in the West of England Trial, down at Newton Abbot but, because of the lubrication problems, I took my ordinary three-fifty instead. So they excluded me for changing my entry at short notice. I told them: "It's a good job I haven't come far, then!"

'Eventually, we found that skimming down the flywheels got over the oiling troubles. But, before then, I rode it in the Inter-Centre Team Trial on a total-loss system, tipping in a quart of oil about every 20 miles. I was determined to get it right, and I did at last, just before the Scott Trial, in which I made best performance on observation.

'Trouble was, a side-valve just hadn't the acceleration to put up a good time in an event like the Scott. Though, in fairness, I must admit it could work up to 70 mph on the road, even on trials gearing.'

Heavy rain on the eve of the British Experts' Trial had made the hills around Stroud, Gloucestershire, extremely muddy and, though the sun had emerged by the time competitors were dispatched from the Bear Inn, on the plateau above the town, the rain was to return in full measure before the day was over. Fortunately, in conditions such as this, riders were allowed to use scrambles-type knobbly tyres—the last major trial to permit this concession.

Jefferies won, with a total of 28 marks lost.

Charlie Rogers (350 Royal Enfield) was runner-up with 35 marks and third man was George Rowley (500 AJS) with 37. And as soon as the results were made known that evening at the Bear Inn, *Motor Cycling* reporter Harvey Pascoe phoned the good news to the home of Edward Turner.

Good news? 'Oh, no; not on a side-valve!' groaned Turner. 'That's the one that shows us least profit.' But Edward was wrong, for Allan's win on such an unusual model gave the Triumph company more publicity than victory on an orthodox bike would have done. Also, the Jefferies model was used as the basis of a new and lighter 500 cc Model 5S side-valve single for the 1939 programme. And that bike, in turn, begat the military 5SW of the early days of the Second World War.

The factory even made and sold a modest number of Allan Jefferies Replicas (the 5S in trials trim) and, notably in Yorkshire, the trials side-valve Triumph got to be quite a fashion for a while. Possibly that was the best Jefferies' practical joke of all, for after the British Experts' Trial he, himself, didn't bother any more with the machine. He had built it simply to prove a point!

Chapter 23

More riders

THE TALE of a lad who, in his first-ever road race, secures a ride on a works model—and scorches home to a well-merited second place—could have come straight from the pages of a schoolboy magazine; except that it happened to be true. The rider was a young Triumph mechanic named **Jack Marshall,** and the race was the first Isle of Man TT of all, in 1907.

Two machines had been specially prepared at the Much Park Street factory but, strictly speaking, they were not official Triumph entries; the entrant's name on the programme was M. J. Schulte but that, of course, was a formality.

Then, as now, TT competitors were to be dispatched from the line in pairs, and it was sheer coincidence that Marshall (No 2) and the other Triumph man, works foreman Frank Hulbert (No 1), were the first competitors to get a TT race under way. Winner of the single-cylinder class of that event was destined to be Charlie Collier (Matchless), but Marshall and Hulbert followed him across the line in second and third places.

If this was indeed Marshall's first road race (as Schulte declared, in a letter to the press), then *Motor Cycle* must have had a good nose for talent, because they had printed Jack's picture, a week before, with a caption line which included: 'of whom much is expected'.

Those expectations came true the following year, when he turned the tables by scoring a TT victory, with Charlie Collier in runner-up position. Jack Marshall came near to repeating that success in 1909, and had worked his way up to a strategic second place when, almost at the end of the race, he was first slowed by a stretching valve then stopped altogether by timing-gear troubles.

After 1910 (when he was sixth, on a Triumph) Jack Marshall withdrew from active competition. But in later years—into the 1950s, indeed—as landlord of the Royal Oak, on Coventry's London Road, he was always ready to stop pulling pints and tell a tale or two of pioneer racing days.

Though he did make several, unsuccessful early TT appearances on Singer and Norton machines, Brooklands was the true stamping ground of **Vic Horsman.** There, he had his own tuning establishment and, from 1922 onwards, he came more and more into prominence in both solo and sidecar racing and, particularly, in record breaking over a variety of distances.

Nominally, his machines were Triumphs, but the upper part of his first engine was unlike anything that ever left Coventry, for it was a two-valve ohv design. With this machine, in 1923, he took the classic hour record at 86.52 mph (it had been held earlier by Frank Halford, development engineer on the Triumph Ricardo project), but when Horsman started the 1924 season, it was apparent that the works had been involved in developing the design.

There was nothing 'home workshop' about the enclosure of the push-rods, or the way in which surplus oil from the rocker gear was led into the primary chaincase. Horsman now had a selection of engines, in 498, 599 and 607 cc capacities (the latter, for attacking certain 750 cc-class records), and with these his bag for the year totalled some 20 records, both solo and sidecar.

Among them again was the hour, which he now lifted to 88.21 mph. Early next year he raised it still more, to 89.13 mph, and though somebody else topped that in October 1925 it was safely back in Horsman's possession only a fortnight later. It now stood at 90.79 mph—and this was the first time that a five-hundred had topped 90 mph for an hour.

Vic Horsman was to leave the Brooklands scene to found a very successful motor-cycle retail business in Liverpool but, as a final salute to his track career, mention just has to be made of the 1926 BMCRC 200-mile Sidecar Race.

In the 600 cc class, 22 machines left the grid. However, as early as the third lap, Horsman, on the Triumph outfit, was in the lead and his most formidable rival, Freddie Dixon (Douglas), had gone out spectacularly with an engine seizure so violent that it had wrenched the rear tyre from the rim.

After 36 laps Horsman led Jack Emerson (HRD) by one lap, with Vic Anstice (Douglas) and George Tucker (Norton) third and fourth but a lap astern of Emerson. By the 42-lap mark, only nine outfits were still circulating. With 60 laps gone, Horsman and Anstice were alone—and then the Douglas driver dropped out with a wrecked engine. That left Vic Horsman by himself, and he lapped with clockwork-like regularity. At 200 miles, and the Triumph credited with a 74.9 mph average, down swept the chequered flag. But Vic Horsman sailed on gaily, and not until he had covered a further 20 miles and 579 yards did he call it a day. The additional distance had given him the three-hour record.

For the 1927 Senior TT, the Triumph factory had decided on a same-as-you-can-buy racing policy and, though there were six official entries, the riders had to do the best they could with standard pistons and compression ratios. Of the six, Wilmot Evans was the only Triumph man to appear consistently on the practice leaderboard.

The race itself was an utter disaster for the works squad, with Tyrell Smith (13th) and Norman Black (18th and last) as the sole survivors. Yet, oddly enough, this same-as-you-can-buy idea was to be justified because into third place came a happy privateer, **Tom Simister,** on a Triumph that he had indeed bought through the normal retail channels.

In a TT career that spanned the years from 1920 to 1931, Simister (a motor-cycle dealer from Macclesfield and, later, Birkenhead) was to ride machines from a variety of companies including, Norton, BSA, Diamond, Velocette and AJS. Also, he was well known in the north as a sand racer at Southport Beach and similar venues.

Interviewed after his 1927 TT third place, he declared himself to be both an 'old man of racing' and a family man. The first claim may, or may not, have been true; the second certainly was, for his son, Jack Simister, was to ride a Triumph into 24th place in the 1950 Senior TT.

Only once did **Freddie Clarke** ride in the Isle of Man and, as with Vic Horsman, he found more satisfaction on the Brooklands bowl. Born in Norfolk in 1911, he made his track début in the 1929 Hutchinson 100, on a 350 cc Montgomery. His first success, on the same machine, came the following year, but soon he had established his own Brooklands tuning shop and was experimenting with Blackburne power units.

He gained his Brooklands Gold Star (for a lap at over 100 mph) on an OEC in 1934, and it was as a result of this that the OEC factory provided him with two machines for the 1935 TT races. In the Lightweight event he ran off course in thick mist, and came to the conclusion that road racing required too much time and concentration. 'As I hadn't the opportunity to do the job thoroughly, I decided it would be better to devote my energies entirely to track work,' he said later.

By 1936 he was track-testing for Ariel, part of the Square Four and Red Hunter development programme, but in his own time he devised a very potent little alcohol-burning 250 cc L2/1 Triumph, of only 51 inch wheelbase and 200 lb weight. At his first attempt he won a three-lap race, but soon he had joined the Coventry firm as assistant development engineer, and pressure of work meant a drastic curtailment of his own race activities.

At Priory Street and, later, Meriden, Freddie was particularly interested in the development of racing engines (to some degree, he was the Doug Hele of his day) and his was the tuning wizardry that brought 1946 Manx Grand Prix success to Ernie Lyons. Freddie was to leave Meriden in 1947, to join Associated Motor Cycles at Woolwich.

The scene changes, and it is now the Thursday afternoon of TT Week in 1972. Into the railed-off enclosure on Douglas Promenade, at the conclusion of the Vintage Club's 'old-course' rally, swings an immaculate 250 cc Tiger 70 in full works International Six Days Trial trim, with a dapper little lady in the saddle.

On that same machine, 33 years earlier, the same lady rider—**Marjorie Cottle,** most famous trialswoman of them all—had made an epic dash for the German frontier when the imminence of war caused the British contingent to make a strategic withdrawal from the 1939 ISDT.

Marjorie first made her name on Raleigh machines. In 1926, for instance, a week after earning a silver award in the Scottish Six Days event, she undertook a publicity ride on a 174 cc model, following a route that, metaphorically, scrawled Raleigh across the map of England. Her marriage in 1927 to road-racer Jack Watson-Bourne was, in the eyes of motor cyclists, the wedding of the year; but she continued to use her maiden name in two-wheel sport.

After competing on a BSA in the 1937 ISDT, Marjorie switched to Triumph for the first time for the following year's event, to be held around Llandrindod Wells, in mid-Wales, and a rather special Tiger 70 was prepared at the factory, incorporating the same modifications as the factory team bikes.

In what was generally acknowledged to have been the most severe ISDT since the series began, she dropped but two marks, and those as the result of being baulked, during the Thursday run, at a long and narrow hill where many of the entry had become bogged down.

Marjorie took the little Triumph to Germany for the 1939 event and then, back in England, it became her everyday wartime transport. For a few years it dropped out of circulation until it was rediscovered, and brought back to showroom condition, by the present owner, Bill Fruin.

Of course (said the pundits) the four-stroke single was the only possible power unit for trials work. Nothing else could produce the right kind of punchy torque. And one might well have gone on thinking that was true—until, in 1946, along came a man who proved that it could all be done on, of all things, a 350 cc Triumph 3T twin.

He was a chartered surveyor from Glastonbury in Somerset, and his name was **Jim Alves.** When he was only 12 years old, he had shown his mechanical aptitude by building a miniature car, with 110 cc engine, at an age when other boys had soap-boxes on pram wheels.

Jim Alves entered the world of trials in 1937 and, on a Velocette, finished with a clean sheet in his first-ever event. That year, however, returning from the Mitchell Trial, he collided with a car. This accident left him with one leg half an inch shorter than the other, though this certainly didn't affect his subsequent career in trials, grass-tracking and scrambles.

He began the 1946 season well, with the 350 cc cup in the Colmore Trial, riding his Velocette. Already the factory scouts had their eyes on him. Eager to see how he would fare, Royal Enfield lent him a works machine for the Victory Trial; and the outcome was another cup for the best 350 cc performance. But Triumph won the race to get Alves' signature on a contract.

The partnership of Alves and the three-fifty twin clicked right from the start, and he had outright wins in three of the first four national trials for which he was entered. From then on, until his retirement from the sport ten years later, he was a member of either the British Trophy or Vase teams in every post-war ISDT except 1947. Indeed, he was to shine even more brightly in long-distance events than in one-day trials, and he was a firm believer in pressing on regardless, and in treating each observed section as it came, with no prior inspection.

'A trial', he claimed, 'loses its essential character if it becomes a series of short rides on easy roads between sections which require only a brief survey for a rider to be successful.'

Although it is for his performances on the 350 cc twin that we remember Jim Alves, in fact he had switched to a 199 cc Tiger Cub long before he hung up his trials boots for the last time.

On the other hand, **Roy Peplow** began his works-riding career on a Cub; and in a very decided manner, by winning the 1957 Bemrose Trial for Triumph. At that time a 21-year-old

signwriter from West Bromwich, Peplow had already been riding a motor cycle for seven years, for the first two years, as joint owner with a schoolmate of a 1930 Raleigh, which he rode round a farmer's field.

Street-legal at last at the age of 16, and with L-plates decorating his 1935 250 cc L2/1 Triumph, he contested his first trial; and finished last, having missed part of the route. But it was a spell of army service that gave his riding the necessary polish for, by good fortune, he found himself under the command of Captain Eddie Dow and in the same squad as Ron Langston.

In khaki, he won one of the rounds of the Army Trials Championship (on a side-valve TRW Triumph twin) and continued by winning the RASC trials championship. Perhaps it was this early spell of military discipline that made him so valuable an ISDT team man in later life. However great the pressures, his riding was always unobtrusive, and his manner cool and unflurried.

The same could be said—and indeed it *was* said—of probably the most dedicated ISDT man this country has yet produced—Hampshire dealer and enthusiast, **Ken Heanes.** He first joined the Trophy squad in 1958, and *Motor Cycle* remarked at the time: 'Son of pre-war trials rider, Jim Heanes, Ken is noted for the calm efficiency with which he deals with mechanical problems'.

Even then, Ken Heanes was an ISDT veteran, for he had first appeared in the event, as a 16-year-old private entry, as far back as 1950. His developing talents as a scrambles rider gained recognition by Triumph, and it was with a specially built 175 cc Tiger Cub that he won a place in the Vase B team of 1956.

From then on, he was an automatic choice as one of the country's ISDT team men and, before making his final bow as a riding member in 1971, he was to be included in the British Trophy sextet on no fewer than 11 occasions.

With the withdrawal of manufacturers' support in 1967, the British riders were left out on a limb, but Heanes was determined that the country should be represented as strongly as possible and, that year, he rode a 504 cc Triumph twin, prepared by himself.

Typical of his initiative and enthusiasm was his personal entry, in 1969, of the only trio which—nominally, at least—represented a British manufacturer. This was his 'Home Counties Triumph' team and, though the effort failed to achieve full success, Heanes himself was to add one more gold medal to his collection.

Going even better, a year later he dipped into his

pocket—and persuaded other dealers to do likewise—to finance the building of 500 and 504 cc Cheney Triumphs for the Trophy team. It was a gallant effort; thwarted though the team was by first-day mishaps (punctures, a leaking fuel tank; it could have happened to anybody), Heanes, the captain, retained his clean sheet throughout. After one last ride in 1971 and one final gold medal, he was at last ready to leave the saddle—but not the ISDT team. Subsequently he became Britain's everywhere-at-once team manager, cheerfully encouraging, dealing with problems as they arose, and ever ready to draw on his vast pool of riding experience.

Riding experience? Even Ken Heanes is a mere novice by comparison with the Peter Pan of the road-race circuits, **Percy Tait.** For many years the chief experimental tester for the Meriden factory, Tait could justly claim to be the most experienced motor cyclist in the world, knocking up a daily average of around 200 miles for something over 20 years.

Between times, he squeezed in a competitions career that had begun (on a Triumph JAP grass-track machine) in 1947, and a spell as a stunt rider with the Royal Signals Display Team. And as if the day wasn't full enough, Percy used to rise at 5 am to tend to his prizewinning pigs!

From time to time, he came into the road-racing limelight with such machines as an NSU, a Ducati and, most surprising of all, a 250 cc two-stroke entered by the Royal Enfield works. Even so, he was still some way from achieving the pinnacle of his racehood.

In a way, it all began to happen for Tait from 1968 onwards, when he was already 37 years old. Around that time Doug Hele and the Meriden development department became interested in the idea of using a modest race programme as an extension of normal experimental work. Tait appeared on the tracks with a businesslike, basically standard 500 cc racer, and works-prepared Bonneville six-fifties were seen in production-machine racing.

Triumph's impact on the racing scene in 1969 was tremendous, and that year's bag included wins in the Production Machine TT and the Thruxton 500-mile race, culminating in the FIM's *Coupe d'Endurance* award for the season. With Bonneville twins and Trident threes, there were more victories to come in the years ahead, with Percy Tait well to the fore.

However, let's return to the 1969 Thruxton 500-mile victory, for in that race Tait shared the saddle with a tallish, forthright Welshman named **Malcolm Uphill,** and he, too, was to write his name in Triumph's racing ledger.

From Caerphilly, Uphill was partly deaf but this, he claimed, was something of an advantage in that he was able to sense the condition of an engine by its feel, and handle it accordingly. He started as a production-class racer (in the 1958 Thruxton 500-miler, where he shared a Tiger 110 with Martin Bourne), and though his later activities included short-circuit and longer-distance racing, his heart remained among the production models.

It was with a Junior-Senior double in the 1965 Manx Grand Prix that Uphill first hit the headlines, but those headlines became bigger still in 1969. There was the Tait-Uphill victory at Thruxton for starters, but the main course was Malcolm's Production-TT win, on a Bonneville twin, at 99.99 mph, with the first-ever production-machine lap at over 100 mph.

Switching to a Trident, he was again Production-TT winner the following year—but by only 1.6 seconds, after a thrilling last-lap scrap with Peter Williams, leading the Norton challenge.

Triumph was well into its racing prime. Still to come were such scintillating performances as those of **Tony Jefferies** (Yorkshire Flyer, Mk II), in taking an 83-bhp Trident to victory in the first Isle of Man Formula 750 event; of **Ray Pickrell**, in winning the 1971 Production Machine TT; and of **Paul Smart** who, with Tait, Pickrell and Jefferies, set the crowds cheering in the superbike championship and Anglo-American match races.

But now the glory was fading. BSA-Triumph cash was fast running out, and for Triumph the race was no longer against Norton, Yamaha and the rest; it was against close-down.

Londoner Pickrell was to score his second Production-TT win in 1972 (and, on the same machine, set a Silverstone race record of 99.39 mph). As mentioned in Chapter 20, this particular Trident was known as Slippery Sam, the only motor cycle in history to win the same Isle of Man TT race in five successive years.

Five years? Yes, indeed, for the venerable Trident collected the silverware yet again, in 1973, 1974 and 1975, bringing laurels for Tony Jefferies, Mick Grant, Dave Croxford and Alex George, as well as for Slippery Sam's owner, Les Williams.

Chapter 24

Way ahead?

AFTER THE FORMAL setting-up of the workers' co-operative on March 6 1975, the men lost no time in making a start. Officially, they got going on the Monday, March 10, with a small workforce clocking in. Even a token batch of 750 cc Triumph twins was wheeled off the assembly line that day. At first, and for some months to come, all machines turned out would be built from those in various stages of completion at the time the factory was closed in the autumn of 1973 by the workers' sit-in. Production from scratch was a long way off. The men had a heavy haul ahead of them, but seemed undaunted.

Meanwhile, output of Triumph Tridents from the Small Heath, Birmingham, plant of NVT was climbing and, in mid-March, the new NT160 model appeared. The engine was inclined forward slightly in the frame, an electric starter was standard, the five-speed gearbox had a left-side change pedal (to comply with safety regulations in the USA), a disc brake was used for the rear wheel as well as for the front, and various other lesser changes were introduced. With its electric starter, five-speed gearbox and disc brakes for both wheels, the NT160 was upsides with the Japanese competition. But, inevitably, the more luxurious specification had to be paid for, and the price came as a shock. It was £1,215, including tax, on the British market. The NT150, without electric starter, sold at £971.

Making the Meriden co-operative work was not just a matter of planning more and more production and increasing the labour force on the shop floor to suit. As the men freely admitted, they had had no experience of management processes and the intricacies of office administration. So they started at the top by engaging a managing director. He was David Jones, 60, formerly director of manufacturing with Jensen, the luxury-car makers.

But, in the broader sense, mid-1975 saw Triumph (or, since the formation of Norton Villiers Triumph, the British industry) at a crossroad. It was not the first crossroad, but was probably the most significant so far faced.

Following the re-creation of a three-factory industry by the setting-up of the Meriden co-operative, the NVT directors had informed the then secretary of state for industry, Anthony Wedgwood Benn, that demand for the current Triumph (and Norton) models could not provide enough work for three factories to operate profitably. This hard fact had been the reason for the Meriden closure in the first place. While trade was booming, NVT could tick over until the Government was ready to talk. However, an economic blizzard had suddenly struck the motor-cycle market in the USA, and had axed big-bike sales. The position had been made even worse by substantial overstocking of Japanese machines, apparently because the 1974 statistics were misread; the marketing experts had mistaken a transient boom, based on a panic to save petrol following the sudden and enormous increase in the price of Middle East oil, for an uplift in real demand.

In 1975 the first quarter's registrations were down by no less than 62 per cent, and Triumph (and Norton) suffered like the rest. The USA was still by far the most important market for British machines, and the recession brought the three-factory argument to a head.

The Government had three choices: stand aside while NVT closed one of its two factories (Birmingham or Wolverhampton); close the co-operative at Meriden; provide NVT with a large investment to pay for a massive engineering effort to develop new models which could be sold in the quantities necessary to keep three factories busy. The investment would be needed also to subsidise losses while the development work was going on and, most important of all, to provide funds for major plant re-equipment.

The last was essential for producing new-generation machines to a very high standard of quality at competitive prices.

The 1½-year delay in resolving the Meriden problem and the final outcome — a daring industrial experiment — had prevented NVT from earning expected profits in 1974 and so restore enough confidence to obtain funds from the stock market for this re-equipment. The Government was, therefore, the only source. If the investment were forthcoming, it would be tantamount to public ownership of NVT and, possibly, the co-operative as well.

At about this time, the Cabinet reshuffle following the Common Market referendum switched Eric Varley to industry secretary in place of Tony

Benn. The distraction in Government circles during the referendum campaign and the change in ministers confused and delayed negotiations even more.

It was now obvious that the vital necessity for survival was an expanded and far more sophisticated engineering programme. British designs had lagged far behind those of other nations, particularly Japan. Nearly every big manufacturer outside Britain was introducing three-, four- or six-cylinder machines, with a wide variety of layouts. Quality and performance were improving by leaps and bounds, particularly in extended maintenance-free mileage. Legislation was enforcing quieter machines and limiting exhaust pollution. Future engine designs would be governed to a considerable extent by the legislative factors.

A new class of relatively wealthy motor cyclist had appeared everywhere — including England, where the old, cloth-cap image dies hard. These riders demanded plenty of good-looking and expensive, though not necessarily essential, equipment. Above all, they insisted on complete reliability and would tolerate only minor maintenance. Rider-felt vibration was taboo.

On the technical side, this was the challenge facing Triumph in 1975. The new-generation machines would have to do better than just meet it. They would, in addition, have to retain the great merit of roadability — top-class roadholding, steering and braking, and a low centre of gravity — on which the reputation of all British machines had been built.

The job could be done, and Triumph could retain its renowned place in the annals of the motor cycle, but only if the funds could be made available to go ahead with a really bold plan of investment for the future.

It was calculated that some £40 million would be needed, partly to pay for development and engineering required to create new models (for Norton as well as Triumph) and, during the period, to sustain work in the Small Heath (Triumph Trident) and Wolverhampton (Norton) factories. The £40 million excluded export guarantees (see Chapter 5) which, at peak periods, would separately have involved around £25 million.

The appeal went unheeded. Mr Varley made his announcement on the day before Parliament closed for the summer recess; he said there would be no reinstatement of ECGD funds for backing exports and no more money for the industry. The NVT Board immediately put into operation plans prepared earlier and an application for liquidation of the Wolverhampton company was made at the beginning of the following week.

A last-minute effort was staged just before the case was heard by holding a meeting on neutral ground (at Kingswinford) attended by the union representatives from Small Heath and Wolverhampton to try to find a way to avoid liquidation and its inevitable consequences. The Wolverhampton men, fired by support from their local MPs, refused to discuss a phased rundown which might be put to creditors with a request to be patient. The men thought the Government could be persuaded to change its mind and, doubtless, that they would be helped to start a workers' co-operative in the Meriden fashion. The meeting was in vain. The Wolverhampton company was in liquidation by Friday, August 7 1975.

In the first instance the Small Heath factory was not affected. By September, though, it was apparent that, because of the joint buying programme under which materials had been ordered in the name of the Small Heath company but for use at Wolverhampton without necessarily making the fact clear to suppliers, the Small Heath company could not avoid liquidation.

However, as the workforce was co-operating fully with the management, Barclays Bank agreed to appoint a receiver and an efficient rundown of the work-in-progress was achieved. This meant the end of production of Tridents and the last models left the assembly line at the turn of the year.

Now, at the beginning of 1978, the future of Triumph rests entirely with the men of Meriden. How far they can succeed depends, basically, on how much financial backing they can get for the new-generation machines which must be introduced to match the competition from Japan, Germany and Italy.

Index